THE NEW
AMERICAN ROAD TRIP MIXTAPE

To Jayson and Nick and Fitz and Becca and Teresa and Sara and Steve and John, who

believed in me before I did.

"This is the story of America.

Everybody's doing what they think they're supposed to do."

— Jack Kerouac, *On the Road*

ASTORIA, OREGON, 8:15 A.M.

I don't know if I'm the only one who thinks that when you set out looking for the big answers in life, you gotta be as uncomfortable as possible when you do it. Seems like, to me, if you're going to have any sort of grand epiphany, it's not going to come while you're sipping mimosas at the Four Seasons or getting a hot stone massage or something.

I stood staring at the newspaper box in front of the Columbia River Coffee Roaster in Astoria, Oregon, under a clearing sky, reading the October 11 *Daily Astorian* headline: "Protestors Occupy Seaside." That was happening, the Occupy Movement. That was now, the time in American history. People remember where they were when Kennedy was assassinated, or on 9/11. During the Occupy movement, I was living nowhere. The previous night had been particularly glamorous.

Raindrops slapped the roof of the station wagon as I tried to sleep in it on the Washington side of the four-mile long concrete-and-steel Astoria-Megler Bridge, my body wedged into a Z-shape on the darker side of the car where a tree partially blocked the light from a streetlamp, trying to ignore the winds rocking the car every few minutes. The humidity was high inside the car, all the windows fogged with seven hours of restless breath.

At 7:30 a.m., I grabbed my toothbrush off the dashboard, stood at the shore with the seagulls for a minute, and scattered a mist of toothpaste spit into the air. I grabbed a half-full water bottle, rinsed my toothbrush and walked over to the restroom, nodding hello to the guy emptying the trash cans. I had a conference call for my job at 9 a.m.

--

October 10 marked 10 weeks of living in my car since the start of my trip, sleeping in a new place every night, finding wireless Internet in coffee shops, libraries, the occasional McDonald's. In less than two and a half months, I had slept in 33 different places: Colorado, Wyoming, Idaho, Utah, Montana, Washington, Oregon, California. This would go on for more than a year, although I didn't know it at the time.

I had left Denver on the last day of July, exactly a month after we broke up. I gave up on marrying her, and we split up our stuff, moved out of our apartment, gave the keys back, and I thought I'd get in some good thinking time out on the road. I'd figure out what was next for me, and when I did, it would be beautiful, heroic, with majestic theme music playing in the

2

background as I drove into another sunset.

When your life plan explodes, you ask yourself big questions. Is there someone for me? Do I even need someone? Do I want a family? Would buying a house, putting down some roots, make me happy? You want a clear answer, and maybe the answer doesn't come all at once, but over several experiences, a dozen conversations, a few thousand miles, a glimpse into a few dozen lives. The ocean, the mountains, the stillness that comes with a couple hours of driving, the unease of not knowing where you're going to sleep each night.

I knew the hip, Generation Y thing to do would have been to get on a plane, go to Europe, India, somewhere more exotic. But my American Dream had dissolved in the middle of a country recovering from a meltdown caused by a mass pursuit of houses with picket fences, and I didn't want to run from it—I wanted to run to it. To me, there was nothing more American than hopping in my car and taking off to drive Out West, hoping something big, something life-altering, something that would make sense of my life, would happen.

It did.

ONE

Tess didn't want a ring; she said she'd rather we spend the money on a trip somewhere instead. Her mother told me to let her know when I was ready to propose and I could use the ring Tess's dad used to propose to her mother almost 40 years ago. At Christmas, her brother said, You know, be careful, because she might actually propose to you. Which meant she had been talking about it with her mother, her sister, and her brother's wife, and that's how he heard.

After almost three years together, you'd think you'd notice things like your girlfriend being too busy to have sex with you the night before she leaves the country for a month, you know, or the distance between you in bed increasing over the past six months. Shit like that. But you don't. Or you do and you deny it because you don't want to believe it.

Sometimes people talk about love as if it's this endless thing, like space. And when a girl tells you she loves you, it's immeasurable, unquantifiable; it feels bigger than anything else you can ever experience. You know what's bigger than that? The space between the meaning of "I love you" and "I love you, but …" That's big, bottomless. It's a fucking ocean.

I should have known when I picked her up at the airport.

She had been gone almost a month in South America. Before I went to the airport, I had showered, cleaned our apartment top to bottom, washed the sheets on our bed, done all our laundry. I had been working out and trying to eat healthier so I'd look good when my girl came back.

In my head, our embrace would be straight out of a movie, right there at the arrivals gate at Denver International Airport. Without words, I would know that she was back, that she had missed me so much she didn't know how she could live without me for that long again. People would give us a tight-lipped smile as they made their way around us and to the baggage claim, an island of love in a sea of weary travelers.

She came to the top of the steps from the terminal shuttle, and I walked around the barrier fence to her. My arms under hers, I pulled her close to me, ready to lift her up off the ground, because I loved the way she laughed when I did that.

She barely wrapped her arms around me. Limp, unenthused, the kind of hug you give your grandmother when you're eight years old and just want to go play in the backyard. It was not the I'm-so-glad-to-see-you hug you get from your girlfriend when she's been away for weeks, when the two of you are young, in love, can't bear to be apart, and can't wait to jump right into bed with each other when you get back to your apartment.

We lasted two more weeks.

--

I had met Tess through a friend of a friend three years before, and I thought it might be okay if I went rock climbing with her, like no one would raise an eyebrow at the fact she was gorgeous and, you know, not my wife, who was at home studying. I think I was trying to fool myself into believing it was totally innocent. But I had a handful of climbing partners, men and women (you can't really climb without someone else on the other end of the rope), and that summer I would have gone climbing with anyone willing to get up early on a Saturday or Sunday and drive the 45 minutes to Eldorado Canyon or the 90 minutes to Rocky Mountain National Park. Tess was five years younger than me and six years younger than my wife. Our third or fourth time on a rope together, I knew I was in trouble.

I was about 20 feet up the feature known as "Cussin' Crack" on a granite formation called Castle Rock in Boulder Canyon, a few miles outside of Nederland, Colorado. The rope hung down from my harness to Tess's hands, and she sat anchored to the rock on a ledge 100 feet off the ground. The rock was slick from almost 60 years of climbing traffic, and handholds were nonexistent. I had read somewhere that I was supposed to employ an old-fashioned move called a "knee bar" at this point, but I didn't know how.

You can tell your brain that it's okay, we're not going to fall, but your brain isn't always able to communicate that to your body. Every time I took my hand off the rock, it quivered wildly. My feet bounced up and down on the tiny footholds, and my heart jackhammered my ribs.

Tess, with her brown eyes and long dark hair that she wore in a braid that hung out of her climbing helmet over the front of her shoulder, slowly paid out rope below, waiting for me to make a move upward or come flying back downward. She was something else, something new, smiling all the time, talking about the months she'd spent in Ecuador and South Africa, and she was years from settling down. But we were just climbing partners, nothing more. I had a lot of climbing partners, both men and women. My wife didn't climb.

I wobbled more, knowing I had a limited amount of time before the muscles in my hands and legs would run out of gas and I'd fall. I did not want to fall — that was the worst thing that could happen in this situation. But hanging on where I was, giving a visual seminar on the human body's response to fear, was humiliating and a close second to falling.

No matter how I tried to rationalize it, I was trying to impress Tess.

We Iowans are sensible people, not rock climbers. Leonard, What the hell would you want to go and do something like that for, I would sometimes imagine my high school football coach saying to me when I was picking my way over a ridgeline while wind gusts tore at my jacket, or looking down at the ground hundreds of feet below as I stepped across onto a foothold the size of a nickel. My wife was from Iowa. Like many Midwesterners who want a slightly taller horizon to look at, we had moved to Denver in our mid-twenties. Still, it wasn't fair for me to ask her to go backpacking in the wilderness, where there was a possibility we'd be eaten by bears — let alone do something as foolish as climbing up a rock face with nothing but a skinny climbing rope to keep her from falling to her death.

But that was where I wanted to be. Up in John Denver's Rocky Mountains, watching the sun set over snowmelt-fed alpine lakes, seeing how tough I really was when I got up high on a climb and things got scary and the weather closed in. I read climbing guidebooks in the bathroom. I found photos of climbs that inspired me and kept a mental tick list of the places I wanted to go: the Grand Teton, Devils Tower, alpine rock climbs all over my adopted home state of Colorado.

My relationship with my wife had been fading since before I started climbing with Tess. Tess climbed and my wife did not. My wife had paralyzing acrophobia, and we were not doing well. All I wanted to do was climb, live out of my car for weeks, and sleep under the stars all over the American West. She wanted a house, a garden and a dog soon, and kids soon after. By early summer, our marriage was a beloved dead oak tree in the backyard that we were working up the courage to cut down.

My wife withdrew, staying in to study every weekend, and I fled to the rock, dragging anyone up routes all over Colorado and Wyoming. I didn't really care if you even knew what to do with the rope; I'd teach you at the base of the climb. Tess and I climbed together a few times, and although I thought she was the most beautiful woman who had ever tied a figure eight knot, I didn't think anyone would notice, what with my desperation to climb with anyone willing.

Tess and I kept it appropriate. Maybe I wondered what it would be like to put my arms around her precipitously curving hips, but the closest I ever got was unclipping gear from her harness while we shared tiny ledges for a couple minutes midway up a climb. More than once, I had watched in awe as she gritted her teeth and clawed her way through a tough move on a climb. For a second, maybe I would imagine what it would be like to roll over in bed on a Saturday morning and ask a woman, "Want to go climbing?" But I was married. Maybe not for much longer, but married.

Somehow I managed to not peel off the Cussin' Crack and cheese-grater myself sliding down the rock face. I didn't lose it, really. I muttered to myself, sweated, and eventually talked myself past the hard part, making my way up the featureless rock thanks only to friction, advances in climbing shoe rubber, and fear of failure. I must have looked like a kid talking himself into jumping into the deep end of the swimming pool for the first time.

At the summit, I sat exhausted on a granite bench, watched the pines on the canyon's south wall calmly rock in the breeze, and took in rope as Tess climbed up behind me, fighting her own battle on the Cussin' Crack. Soon enough, she pulled over the last move to the ledge and gave me a look of relief, and I looked into her eyes and knew I was in trouble. This was a woman who loved what I loved, and I was not in love with my wife anymore.

Tess tied herself into the anchor and sat next to me. I tried to not wish she was sitting closer and tried to not wish she was holding my hand. I busied myself piling the rope at my feet instead of putting my arm around her.

Tess went to Mexico for the rest of the summer. A month later, I came back from a trip to the Tetons and my wife was sleeping on the couch. We filed no-contest divorce papers and the next morning, I took off and did my first ropeless climb, the 1,000-foot East Face of the Third Flatiron above the city of Boulder, and at the top vowed to never do it again. Tess and I wrote letters and e-mails, never quite saying what we were really thinking about each other.

I moved into a 400-square-foot studio apartment in Capitol Hill, all windows on the east side, lots of sunshine. I fell in love with Tess there. I remember the first few weekends we spent together after she returned from Mexico. I had imagined we'd be off climbing, sleeping in a tent all the time; but it was late fall and Denver had some bad weather. We slept in on Sundays, sometimes until the early afternoon. I was so tired from the emotional turmoil of getting divorced, and I could hold her forever, even with all that daylight pouring in the east window.

I didn't care that we weren't out climbing. I was so happy. I thought, "THIS is what it's supposed to feel like." I would lie next to Tess and put my hand on one of her cheeks and kiss the cheek closest to me, and it felt so good. Like it was what I'd been waiting for my entire life. I watched her sleep, and I didn't need anything else.

--

The last time I ever saw her, she walked away from me and into the terminal at DIA to get on a plane to Quito. I shuffled through the rain to the car at the Departures drop-off, exhausted, wiping tears off my face.

Back when we thought we were happy a few months prior, or at least when I thought we were happy, I had dropped $1,500 on my own plane ticket to Quito, where I would meet her for two weeks in Ecuador. Then we'd fly back to the U.S. and have more adventures, climbing, sleeping under the stars, running through the mountains somewhere, before she took off to New York for another job in the fall and I followed her there.

I didn't give a shit about the money, about the plane ticket when I canceled it, about not getting to see Ecuador. When we first got together, I told her to follow her heart, take seasonal jobs that don't pay much but allow you to work in the mountains, live your dream and I'll worry about paying the rent, because I always wished someone would have done that for me so I could become a writer. Because if you love people, you help them. You take care of them. You give give give to make them happy because you love it when they smile, and that's love, isn't it?

I sat there in the car at the terminal, watching the windshield wipers fan back and forth for a minute in the dark, and all I knew was that something was wrong with me, and that's why she didn't want me anymore. I put the car in first gear to drive 40 minutes back to a Capitol Hill apartment that had a bunch of girls' stuff in it, but no girl.

I couldn't stay in Denver. I needed to go. Somewhere. I couldn't sit around and think about it, spend another month in that hot, miserable apartment, going out to dinner at the restaurants she and I went to, sitting in the same coffee shops I had sat in for six months, overworking myself at a laptop, staring out the window and wondering why.

--

In the mailbox at our apartment was a postcard from Costa Rica, where she had been back on June 2, and still loved me. It said so in the salutation: "Hola mi amor!"

The postcard got to me a little more than three weeks later, after the tepid hug at the airport, after the awkward days of her being home, and just before she told me that it might be better if we broke up. The pace of international mail is cruel.

It was over no matter what I said or did—she just hadn't said so yet. We had awkwardly stumbled through 11 days of too-quiet dinners, 11 nights of me trying to hold her as she went to sleep and her letting me but never putting her arms around me. I'm not sure about us, she kept saying, I'm just not sure. I'm not sure.

I grinded out a trail run on Green Mountain, a tremendous grassy hill on the west side of Denver just before the big mountains begin, as the sun started to set. I wanted the pain. The first mile of trail is so steep, it takes me 17 minutes to run it, lungs and heart redlining the whole time, gasping for air, calves and thighs burning. I pounded up the hill, barely running, barely able to breathe the whole way up, wondering if I could make it. It was brutal, as always. If I didn't have that trail to run, I might have just asked someone to hit me with a baseball bat a few times.

I popped over the top of the mountain after 19 minutes and started the rolling terrain down and around the rest, another 60 minutes of running for me. The city and the suburbs rolled out in front of me as I ran the top of the peak, and the sun dropped low over the mountains, softening everything around me. The long grass swayed in a low breeze, and for a minute it wasn't the hottest and saddest summer I'd spent in Denver, and I loved the top of this big grassy lump in the foothills.

Days like this I could run forever up here. It was like I was on a cloud. She wasn't going to stay; I knew it in there somewhere. And for a minute up on the trail, that was OK.

--

She wanted to see the world, and I had bought a ticket to Ecuador to show her I wanted to do it with her. It would have been my first trip outside the U.S., the first stamp in the passport I'd gotten a month earlier at age 32—way too old to have a blank international travel resume, I'd always thought. Some kids graduated college and spent a month backpacking in Europe. I didn't do that. I hadn't been to Patagonia or Nepal, or even Mexico. When she talked about why we maybe weren't right for each other, Tess pointed to my lack of appetite for traveling to other countries. I said, Give me a chance, I just haven't been anywhere yet, maybe this trip will wake me up, get me excited to go other places.

But was that the truth? We broke up. I canceled my plane ticket to Ecuador, which gave me enough airline credit to go plenty of places. I could climb in Italy, in the Dolomites, fly to Dublin and explore the city, write somewhere for a week or two. I should go somewhere, shouldn't I? Stamp my passport, do something to remedy my travel resume, which looked like that of a true small-town Iowan. I had long been secretly ashamed of it, my un-worldliness. Whenever party conversations turned to others' experiences in foreign countries, I just listened, hoping no one would ask me, Brendan, have you ever been anywhere?

Now was the perfect time. Relationship over, I could go somewhere, somewhere fantastic, show Tess, or maybe even just spite her a little bit. Italy, Ireland, hell, Iceland, India?

I packed my car. I wanted to leave from my house, not jump on a plane and be dropped somewhere, passing the journey inside a climate-controlled cabin with air pumped in. My friend Mick, then 50, said something to me a couple summers ago about how he wanted to start big trips from his driveway, a few miles down a dirt road off I-25 south of Denver. Then he borrowed my bike trailer and pedaled 1,800 miles to his hometown near Lansing, Michigan. He biked through Iowa, Nebraska, Illinois, and Wisconsin, and he was as excited about the trip as any he'd taken to New Zealand, Costa Rica, or Baja. Leaving from his driveway.

I could buy that plane ticket to Dublin or Milan or wherever next year.

I had been driving all over the West since I was 24, watching the great mountains and endless deserts pass by my car windows as my mind wandered, seven or nine days at a stretch. I didn't want to fly halfway around the world, see the Eiffel Tower, the Colosseum, or whatever. I felt better placing a bet on driving west, trying to paint on a familiar canvas. I would still be the only person I knew who had never been anywhere, failed to exercise my right as middle class bourgeoisie.

I had an atlas at my apartment that I'd kept since 2002, highlighting every stretch of road I'd driven in every western state — miles of roads in Colorado, Wyoming, Montana, Idaho, Washington, Oregon, California, Nevada, Utah, Arizona, and New Mexico. Thousands of miles of bright yellow and pink tracing, dozens of adventures, dozens of sunsets and sunrises in the desert and the mountains, hundreds of hours with friends, solving our problems from the front seats of the car, everything we needed packed in it for a week or more. Every time I started down a new highway somewhere, I said to myself, "This is new highlighter."

Everyone in this country should be able to look at a map and see places they want to visit, dots they can mark on that map. Plenty of us have passions that can connect those places. Maybe we want to see a game in each of the three great baseball stadiums in the East: Fenway Park in Boston and Shea Stadium and Yankee Stadium in New York. Maybe we have four different rivers we want to fly-fish in Montana, Idaho, and Wyoming. Maybe it's a tour of wineries in Napa and Sonoma counties in California, or microbreweries in the Pacific Northwest. Maybe we just want to visit all of our brothers and sisters, spread out all over the country.

My map is a collection of climbing destinations, wilderness areas and national parks, places I wanted to go to see natural beauty, feel small, and maybe stand on top of something. I've been to the places I've been because I saw a photo of a certain mountain or lake or trail, or heard about it somewhere, and packed a backpack and drove there.

When Tess left, I had nothing keeping me in Denver. Could I go out and bring something back from the mountains, maybe something worth sharing? I didn't need a Lonely Planet book or a travel magazine article to figure out where I wanted to go. I didn't want to go sightseeing.

Eight years before, a guy had been climbing up the Southwest Ridge of Borah Peak, the highest mountain in Idaho, talking to my friend Tim and me about his recent travels Out West from his home in Pennsylvania. All I remember he said was, "People out on the East Coast, they spend all this time flying to Europe, and they've never once been out here and seen all this." He looked out over the Lost River Range and the thousands of acres of the Challis National Forest below us and waved his hand over all of it.

--

Half the scroll was rolled out in a 60-foot-long glass case, waist-high. One of the clerks on the fifth floor of the library said it was not, in fact, butcher paper, but teletype paper, and she told me I was too young to remember what that was. It was 2007 and I was 28, and not quite too young. I stood above the glass case, trying to comprehend 56 years ago in literary history along with 13 years of my own history since I bought my first and only copy of *On the Road*. There were no paragraph breaks in the first draft, and it was yellowed with age. The librarian said the scroll was incredibly brittle when she helped roll it out into the glass case.

It was the fiftieth anniversary of the book's publication, and the library had gotten a hold of the entire 120-foot original manuscript and laid it out in the Western History and Genealogy section on the top floor of the Denver Public Library. I just walked across the street from my office one day on a lunch break, took the elevator up and stood in front of my own Shroud of Turin. And nothing really happened, just that small but final feeling you get when something clicks into place and closes a circle in your life.

The sheets of teletype were taped together by Kerouac himself, prior to his 20-day marathon from April 2, 1951 to April 22, 1951, so he wouldn't have to keep stopping to put in a fresh sheet of paper. That tape was almost 56 years old, and Kerouac died when he was 47.

I stood there with my old beat-up paperback, looking at the scroll, trying to ask a long-dead literary hero for his autograph. I flipped open my book and compared the first paragraph to the words Kerouac had typed on the scroll:

I first met Neal not long after my father died...I had just gotten over a serious illness that I won't bother to talk about except that it really had something to do with my father's death and my awful feeling that everything was dead. With the coming of Neal there really began for me that part of my life that you could call my life on the road.

In my copy:

I first met Dean not long after my wife and I split up. I had just gotten over a serious illness that I won't bother to talk about, except that it had something to do with the miserably weary split-up and my feeling that everything was dead. With the coming of Dean Moriarty began the part of my life you could call my life

19

on the road.

I was 15 when I bought my copy of the book. I picked it up in a shopping mall bookstore and read the first 20 pages before I made myself stop reading to go pay for it. My hometown, New Hampton, was small, 3,000 people, and my high school was known more for its football and wrestling teams than it was for its fine-arts curriculum. I first heard of *On the Road* in someone's biography, and I remember it just sounded like the grandest fairy tale that a lost teenage kid could hear of.

The book opened up a world outside my quiet, desperate, small-town bubble, as it probably did for most young people who read it. By the end, Kerouac was my hero. I wanted to be Sal Paradise, and I couldn't imagine how people could go their entire lives without reading Kerouac's frenetic prose.

When I was 17, I used *On the Road* to pick up a girl at my high school, leaving it in her locker with instructions to please read it and call me with her thoughts on it. She did, and we dated for four months, breaking up the summer before I left for college. She gave me the book back.

I read a life list of other books in college instead of studying for the marketing degree that I barely earned. I discovered Hunter Thompson, *Slaughterhouse Five, A People's History of the United States, Zen and the Art of Motorcycle Maintenance, Love in the Time of Cholera, Catch-22* and dozens of others.

I hunted for used Hemingway paperbacks on the shelves of thrift stores, and I joined a bunch of those book-of-the-month clubs so I could get eight free books right away.

When I moved to Montana when I was 23, I left most of my books back in Iowa. I never considered abandoning my beat-up paperback copy of *On the Road.* Then. leaving Montana after graduate school, I sold or gave away as much as possible, ditching all my "furniture" and paring my book collection down to the smallest single box I could fit in the car. When I left Missoula for Phoenix, I convinced my friend Nick to come with me, and we took the first real road trip I'd ever been on, dirtbagging it down the Pacific coast, flying through eight states in a little more than 10 days, camping when we could, and a couple times spending uncomfortable nights sleeping in the car. When my girlfriend and I left Phoenix for Denver a year later, I once again had to chop my pile of books down. Sal and Dean of course made the cut.

By the time *On the Road* turned 50, I was 28, and still had my first copy. The legend was that Kerouac had written the entire first draft of the book on a giant scroll of butcher paper flowing through his typewriter, popping Benzedrine and frantically hammering away for 20 days in 1951. Like many great books, it almost didn't get published; but it did in 1957, and stayed popular enough that I could find it in a Midwestern bookstore in 1995 and have it knock me on my teenage ass. There was something to it, the romance and adventure of the road before the Interstate Highway System completely crisscrossed the country, to the laments of all those who liked to see something when they drove in their cars.

Thomas McGuane, in an essay about Kerouac, once wrote, "He trained us in the epic idea that ... you didn't necessarily have to take it in Dipstick, Ohio, forever. ... Kerouac set me out there with my own key to the highway."

Plenty of us come from Dipstick, Ohio, or Dipstick, Wherever. That passage of McGuane's hit home for a kid from Dipstick, Iowa, 17 years after reading Kerouac's book, living on the highway. If you ever get famous as any sort of artist, people ask you who your influences are, meaning whose art do you channel in some way, whose work has pushed your work in the direction it goes. I don't know if anyone will ever ask me that question, but if they do, I don't know if I could say Jack Kerouac's writing influenced my writing. The influence, apparently, has been on my life. Maybe not so much the words that come out on the paper, but where I've gone to find the words.

--

Page 37 of the September 2011 issue of *Outside Magazine* has a box titled "Triggering Events," listing five ways "How nuclear road trips begin." Number 1: "Career change—voluntary or involuntary. Number 2: "Acceptance to grad school." Number 3: "Breakup." That issue, with a cover story about road trips, appeared on newsstands just as I started to pack my car in front of my apartment in Capitol Hill to leave town for A Few Weeks or Who Knows Maybe Longer.

I sent text messages, a few e-mails to friends, climbing partners: What are you doing in August? Brian, Teresa, Tommy. Let's go to Idaho, Banff, climb something. People said yes. A loose plan began to form. I checked in with other friends: I might be coming through town, Missoula, Seattle, Salt Lake City, Portland, sometime in August. You busy? Nah, come on by. We have a couch or a guest bedroom or a floor. Great. I applied for a Writer's Residency at the Banff Centre, at the foot of the Canadian Rockies. I got in. I would sit there and write for a week, like a real writer. Turning lemons into lemonade.

I mentally scanned a map of the West in my head. Where were my friends, people I always said I would visit when I got the time? I said it in my head, then out loud: I'm going on a climbing trip, and afterward, I think I might couch-surf down the West Coast. I'll just do it until I stop having fun, and then I'll come back to Denver and settle back in. That was the plan. Of course, then, I didn't know what was going to happen to me.

I had lunch with an old friend in Denver, explaining the plan to her, and I said it out loud at the table: I'm going to spend five weeks living out of my car and climbing, and then I'll drive down the coast and see some friends, see how long I can live on the road.

She said, "That sounds like *Eat, Pray, Love*, for men."

Elizabeth Gilbert's *Eat, Pray, Love*, a tremendously bestselling book, took her around the world for a year, learning how to enjoy life, find spirituality, and fall in love again after a failed marriage and ensuing rebound relationship. Of course, she had signed an advance book deal that paid for the whole trip. I didn't have a book deal. I had a stack of rejection letters from a book manuscript I'd been trying to sell for three years.

The American road-trip legend is held high by a handful of great works, and writers have been hitting the road to begin the literary process since before the Interstate Highway System. Jack Kerouac wrote *On the Road*; John Steinbeck wrote *Travels with Charley*. William Least Heat Moon spent three months on the road after splitting up with his wife and losing his job, covering 13,000 miles and writing *Blue Highways*, his first book. Robert Pirsig's *Zen and the Art of Motorcycle Maintenance* covered a 17-day motorcycle trip from Minnesota to California. Steinbeck figured on covering 10,000 or 12,000 miles. Ten thousand miles sounded good. Is that what you need to figure out what you want out of life?

None of those guys were Lewis and Clark—none of them were exploring any place that hadn't already been explored by someone else. But they all found new stories to tell.

So much of American culture draws from the road: Dennis Hopper and Peter Fonda in *Easy Rider,* the movie that sold a million motorcycles. Susan Sarandon and Geena Davis in *Thelma & Louise. Fandango. Smokey and the*

Bandit. Into the Wild. Songs like Bob Dylan's *Tangled Up in Blue.* Willie Nelson, *On the Road Again.* Johnny Cash, *I've Been Everywhere.* Simon & Garfunkel, *America.* The Allman Brothers, *Ramblin' Man.* Led Zeppelin's *Ramble On.* But it's been a while since anyone had made something classic, really classic, about The Road. Hasn't it? Is our romance with the highway a relic of a previous generation?

Maybe I still wanted to believe that driving out into the wide open and staring off into it for a while was good for something, that it could be powerful, healing, whatever happens. Could we still believe in the mythical American road trip?

Early in *On the Road*, Kerouac writes:

What did it matter? I was a young writer and I wanted to take off. Somewhere along the line, I knew there'd be girls, visions, everything; somewhere along the line, the pearl would be handed to me.

Fifteen-year-old me was still in there somewhere, believing it and itching to take off.

My America wasn't Kerouac's or John Steinbeck's; it wasn't post-war or baby boom or Cold War or any of those unifying things—it was post-housing bubble, post-economic downturn, post-greed. We were all trying to figure out what went wrong to make the economy collapse on us.

When the housing market crashed in 2008, many Americans realized they were too leveraged into mortgages they couldn't afford because they were on a graduated repayment schedule and their raises at work hadn't exactly matched up with the increases in their mortgage payments. Or they lost their homes, or they lost their jobs and then lost their homes. People in my neighborhood moonlighted delivering pizzas in $30,000 cars — sometimes, I presumed, just to make the monthly payments on those cars.

Houses trapped lots of people close to me. My brother couldn't accept a transfer for a different job in his company because he couldn't sell his house in Wisconsin, no matter how many times he dropped the price. Another friend bought as much house as he could for the money he had, and when his wife was laid off, was totally under the gun to make a payment on a huge, empty house 45 minutes from downtown, way out in the suburbs. They had closed on the house on the eve of the housing bubble bursting, their interest rate literally increasing every day, and he later told me that he wished someone would have told them to Hold on, take a deep breath, make sure this is what you want to do. Because now they were in over their heads. Another friend who had spent four years improving his house in a hip neighborhood admitted defeat. He said they were "just hoping to get out of it what we put into it" when they finally closed on the sale, a few weeks before his wife gave birth to their first child. People said things like, "When the housing market rebounds, we're going to sell this place and …"; but nobody knew when the housing market was going to rebound. Other dreams were on hold.

I saw people who missed opportunities to go somewhere else, to go after a better career opportunity or a better place in America, because they had a $200,000 anchor holding them down, a home that two years before would have made them a nice profit when they packed up and left. A home that everyone told them they needed to buy in order to be an adult. Come on, think about the pride of home ownership; you're throwing your money away paying rent; don't you want a garage, a lawn, a place you own? And it had backfired on so many people who thought they were doing the right thing, building equity, putting down roots, getting some stability.

So I guess it seemed like as good a time as any to move into my car for a while.

--

Tess had decorated the refrigerator door with photos of us, maybe a dozen in all. I tugged two of them from underneath magnets, the ones I liked, and put them in a file box, not sure what I would ever do with them or when I would look at them again. In one of the photos, taken in a Utah slot canyon on Thanksgiving two years before, I really liked her smile. She looked happy, maybe happy to be in such a beautiful place, or happy to be there with me.

I wrapped up the last weeks of work, gradually cleaning the things that were mine out of the apartment — skis, tents, computers, books, was this book mine or hers, my photos, gifts my friends had given me — keeping only the stuff I absolutely needed. I pulled my cork board off the wall, filled with all the snail-mail rejection letters I'd accumulated over the years trying to sell my book manuscript about how rock climbing saved my life after I finished rehab. The four different titles I'd given it spelled out the desperation: *The Only Good Story I Know, Hanging On, The 13th Step, Sixty Meters to Anywhere.*

The dishes were hers, a gift from her family. I had gotten rid of mine when we moved in together. Didn't matter anyway, since there were only a couple plates and bowls I had picked up at a thrift store after my wife and I divorced and I told her to keep the dishes. Fiesta Ware, both sets, both gone to women after breakups. This was getting to be a recurring theme. We split up, they say "nothing's really wrong," and I have no dishes. Pots and pans, she could keep.

I tried to be emotionless, ruthless. I didn't care; keep all this shit. The bed was a gift from her mother, keep it. Couch, same thing. Kitchen table. Dresser. End table. Fuck, I had nothing. I didn't want anything. I kept my roll-down classroom map that hung above her couch, that I always wanted showing the page of the United States and my beloved West, and that she always wanted to flip to show the world map on the next page.

I ferried a couple car loads to a friend's storage unit. Pretty soon, I was down to one carload: climbing gear, two cameras, laptop, some street clothes, many more mountain clothes, crampons, camp stoves, tent, sleeping bag. That would go with me.

--

My Iowa hometown had six stoplights when I was growing up there in the nineties, no Starbucks, no McDonald's, let alone a movie theater. Friday and Saturday nights, starting at age 15, if I didn't have to work as a dishwasher and busboy, I drank beer in someone's car rolling down one of the gravel roads of Chickasaw County, which lined the farm fields north-to-south and east-to-west, a grid with one-square-mile plots of corn and soybeans in between.

We drove around for hours, guzzling from cans of Busch Light and Old Milwaukee as quickly as possible, only stopping to pee in the middle of the road. We'd see maybe four or five cars per hour, fewer later in the night. We needed a place to get away from our parents, the gossip-hungry eyes of our small town, and the cops. Our sanctuary was usually a rusted-out '85 Cutlass Ciera or Sunbird, where we could listen to Pearl Jam and wish we had prom dates. In the vernacular of New Hampton High School, this was called "road tripping." We didn't exactly have what you'd call vision.

I had almost graduated from high school before a buddy made an observation about my gravel-road driving:

You know, there's no point in going faster than 35, said whoever it was, as we were rolling down another cornrow-straight dirt road, holding beers between our legs.

What do you mean, I asked.

Well, it's not like we're trying to get somewhere, he said.

But we were. We just had nowhere to get to.

My last time back in Iowa visiting my parents, I caught myself driving 85 mph in a 55 mph zone in a rental car, flying down a country road somewhere in the dark. I had no reason to be in a hurry; I was just going fast without realizing it.

I used to do that in college, and during high school too. I'd drive somewhere late at night, listening to music, smoking a cigarette or spitting chewing tobacco juice into an empty soda bottle, and I would just *floor it*, sometimes driving down an empty county road with my headlights off, using only moonlight to watch the lines on the road. And there I was again, in my thirties, in a rental car driving away from the Des Moines airport, nowhere to be, but flying anyway at 85 mph.

It was something about the landscape there that made me itchy, fidgety, restless. I was desperate to go. Maybe always had been.

--

I imagine every man who does an Internet search for the phrase "average sex frequency" does it in the middle of the night, after tossing and turning next to a sleeping, fully-clothed girlfriend or wife who said something like Not Tonight a couple hours before. Tess and I had talked about what was enough, and if we were talking about it, I should have realized that some sort of spark was gone. Nobody's that tired all the time. I should have seen it

30

coming.

After she brought it up, I could see that our relationship had problems, yes, but I never saw them as deal-breakers or show-stoppers, just things we "needed to work on." Yes, I didn't share her same passion for travel, and I was more focused on my career than she was on hers, and I didn't want to leave the city for a small town in the mountains.

There's no word for the feeling when you know something is coming, know know know as sure as the sun's going to go down at the end of the day; but when it happens, it still shocks you. A few days prior, I was a man in his early thirties with a slightly younger girlfriend, still feeling young despite some aching joints, the occasional gray hair, and deepening lines on my face—and I was perfectly comfortable with loving one woman for the rest of my life.

The day after she broke up with me, I was a man who might never meet another woman; might never have children; and, after we split up our stuff, would again be without a stick of furniture or a set of pots and pans, sad and pathetic in my failure to acquire any material goods that signified a typical, stable middle age.

I didn't want to reconsider what I wanted in a partner, what type of woman I wanted to date. I didn't even want to go on dates. I wanted to work on our relationship, not break up, and when I said that out loud, I was surprised at how good I thought it sounded.

I walked around with a brick in my stomach, cried at night by myself in bed, trying to wring my sadness out like it was dirty water in a sponge. I wondered how she could fall out of love with me, just like that, and my feelings hadn't changed.

Then I saw this photo. Maybe it was a magazine ad for cologne or something—a woman with her arms around a man's neck, both of them smiling, maybe she was even laughing. They were so close, her elbows were next to his ears, her wrists crossed behind his head.

When was the last time she did that to me? Sure, she was gone for a month for work, and when she came back for two weeks, she never touched me, saying she was thinking about a lot of heavy stuff. Then we had a we-need-to-talk talk, and another one, and another one, and then she said it was over. I started to have trouble remembering a moment in the last six months when I felt really loved.

Is this what happens to every relationship? You're together two or three years and you become lazy with your affection? You never sneak up behind your boyfriend or girlfriend in the kitchen and wrap your arms around them anymore? You roll to the other side of the bed, sleep becoming more important than holding someone close to you? No more spontaneous kisses on the top of the head?

I didn't want that.

I realize our sex drive wanes throughout life, throughout

relationships. But was it too much to ask to have someone who just maybe might want to pull my clothes off in the kitchen every once in a while, letting the pasta boil over or the potatoes burn because we're too busy exploring a non-food, non-work, non-sleep, non-computer need?

I'm a man; I'm not 22 anymore. I understand cellulite; I understand that women go number two, that you like to wear sweatpants sometimes, that a couple times a year I will get to take care of you when you have a fever and snot dripping into your mouth and a pile of used tissues next to you on the bed. I understand that you get bloated before your period, that you are human, and not a photoshopped creation in a "Men's Interest" magazine.

Cellulite is fine. Sweatpants are fine. You can snore, sleep with your mouth open. You can take all those moments of your life that you are not sexy, and you can multiply them all by 100 and add them together, and they disappear when I'm lying behind you and I put one hand on your hip and kiss the back of your neck.

While I was trying to do everything right in our relationship, I should have noticed her slipping away. That it wasn't about anything I was doing wrong, the clothes I was wearing, the extra five or 10 pounds that came and went with the seasons, about her being tired or stressed or having indigestion or having to get up early the next morning. It was about us. It was about us not being perfect for each other, despite how much of myself I poured into it.

Enough times of "not tonight" finally adds up to "not with you." I was just too dumb to do the math along the way.

--

I started to make a mental list while driving I-80 across Wyoming, then pulled a piece of paper out of the glove box and started scribbling on it, using the fat part of my steering wheel as a writing surface. I'm 32 years old. This car has 200,700 miles on the odometer. I have a few gray hairs poking through. I have crow's feet, a few forehead lines, some other smile lines on my face. Two weeks after my girlfriend broke up with me, I found out my ex-wife was pregnant with her first child, due sometime around the third anniversary of the day we went down to the Denver City and County Building and filed our divorce papers. Now I'm leaving on a trip, and nobody's waiting for me to come home, and I don't have a home now anyway.

--

I don't have a bed, I repeated to myself in the car as I watched flat, open Wyoming roll by on I-80. I was headed for the town of Green River, 370 miles from my old apartment and would arrive hopefully shortly after dark. I don't have a couch either, or pots and pans, a kitchen table, all the basics of an American family home. I have about five grand in a savings account, three grand or so in an IRA, and roughly $50,000 in student loan debt.

But no mortgage, no car payment, no 90 days Same-As-Cash payment due on a sectional sofa or a washer and dryer, no property taxes due, no second vehicle or second home, no gym membership, no utility bill, no Internet bill. I had written the last rent check already. It was the end of something.

I can fall in love with any landscape when it's bathed in the golden sunlight of the last two hours of the day, I said to myself, drumming my fingers on the steering wheel as I passed the rocks of Vedauwoo between Cheyenne and Laramie. Starting with Wyoming. There was a little hope riding along in the car somewhere.

TWO

My first night without a bed, "my" bed, a bed to miss like you sometimes do when you're somewhere else, I lay on the floor of Brian's furnitureless living room in Green River, Wyoming, with a 1-inch-thick camping pad under my sleeping bag. On my back, looking up at the ceiling, thinking, "Denver was where I used to live," I fell dead asleep. At 2:30 a.m., the sound of someone vomiting in the parking lot outside snapped my eyes open and for a moment I didn't know where I was.

Brian worked for the summer as the leader of a team that inspected boats for species of invasive mussels at the Flaming Gorge Reservoir, the most serious he'd gotten about working since I'd known him. He was 28, and the Green River apartment marked the first time I could remember that he had an actual address and I didn't have one.

Brian is from Tallahassee, a world traveler, the kind of guy who would sell all his stuff and take a job teaching English in China for the free plane ticket that came with it, like he did in 2008. I called him "alpha dirtbag" for his ways of making money out of nothing—finding a rechargeable lithium battery for a power drill at a Goodwill store, buying it for $5, then selling it on eBay for $75. Or buying a Honda Civic for $500 in Florida, driving it to Colorado, driving it around all summer, and then selling it for $800 without so much as paying for an oil change.

He has red hair, a red beard, never talks over anyone, plays the banjo and the guitar, loves being from the South but loves mountains too, and was in a holding pattern that summer in Green River, trying to convince the Coast Guard to accept him into its officer training school. He had no military experience, but had a master's degree in human geography from the University of Edinburgh. He had a hard time getting a job in Denver the previous winter, and he was looking to get a job that would put some leadership experience on his resume. Even if that job was in Green River, Wyoming, where I woke up on the floor the next morning.

Brian and I sweated under the last-day-of-July sun heading into Idaho in the Subaru, cutting across the dry, brown high desert of western Wyoming. I had a mountain to climb, a friend to talk to, and enough sweat to fill a beer bottle. I only wished I had gotten the air conditioner fixed when someone else was in the car with me. We rolled the windows down, turned up Waylon Jennings's "Are You Sure Hank Done It This Way," turned it up more until it was too loud to hear each other speak, then pumped our fists out the windows in time with the song as we passed semis rolling west on I-80, because that's how you start a road trip.

--

When the repair estimates got higher than $1,000, and they did every once in a while, I liked to ask Baki, If this were your car, would you do it? Just to see what he'd say. The way he answered—and he always said yes—I think he did think my Subaru was kind of his car, too—even though it was ugly and had enough dents and dings in the body that I'd tell people the car was "its own burglar alarm." One time a mechanic said Yeah, I've seen hundreds of these go 200,000 miles, and plenty of them, probably a few dozen, go 300,000. Stuff like that, I started to believe in my car like my mom believed in Jesus—it ran on faith; I didn't need science or evidence. Plus, I mean, there's something really un-American about buying a new car for an old-fashioned road trip, I think.

I bought my 1996 Subaru Outback Impreza in 2006, the year after I had moved to Denver and a couple weeks after a guy smashed my old car in an accident. It was $4,000 and had 136,000 miles on it, a few dents, a couple holes from cigarettes in the seats. But it had rubber floormats, a back seat that folded down, and just enough room for a 5'11" me to lie down in the back of it. It had all-wheel drive to get me up to the mountains during the winter and high enough ground clearance to get me up most reasonable Forest Service roads in the mountains and most decent roads in the desert.

At the time, it also had a working air conditioner, rear defrost, all four speakers, no problems with the paint, and an immaculate windshield.

Baki called from the garage in Denver. He said it would be about $1,700 to replace both the transmission and clutch. He said I could keep their loaner car overnight. Jesus Christ, I thought, Should I dump $1,700 into a $4,000 car? I didn't exactly have the money, but I didn't have the money to buy a new car, either.

I asked Baki, If this were your car, would you do it?

"Yes," he said. "I would do it. We'll get some more miles out of this car. It has a good motor."

So they did it. Sliding my credit card for $1,700 was a commitment to the car. The next day, the A/C compressor started making a loud puffing noise, even when I just wanted to use the defrost. Shit. They had told me a couple years back that one day the compressor would just blow up, shooting pieces of itself into the air conditioning system, and requiring that the entire system be replaced. I called Baki. Baki, I said, I just dumped $1,700 into this car, and replacing the A/C compressor is another $1,300.

"Yeah, bring it in," he said. "Can you come down today?" I drove to the shop.

I walked in the front door, and Baki and I turned around and walked out. I opened the hood, and he reached in and unplugged the power to the compressor.

"There you go," he said. "Now it won't turn on. When you get some money, you bring it in and we'll get it fixed." We shook hands.

When Tess left me, the Subaru had just turned over 200,000 miles. The average new-car buyer trades in their car when it reaches 55,000 miles, or after about four years of driving. Should I get rid of mine, get something newer, make some car payments? I hadn't had a monthly car payment since 2004. Think about it: Air conditioning. Rear defrost. The new(er) car smell — something other than dirt, sweat, and climbing gear. I'd be able to roll over potholes and hardly feel them.

Hell no, I thought. I wanted to drive it till it quit on me, like a horse that just can't go anymore. I wanted to make a statement about consumption, recycling, consumerism, and all that stuff, even though no one would notice or care. To other people, it was just another beat-up car on the road. But it was important to me, and important to Baki.

I got one last oil change and vacuumed it out for one last time before I packed it with all my stuff.

As I hopped on I-25 North to leave Denver, I was sweating. My ass was hot, my back was hot, and a trickle of sweat rolled down my sternum. The vent blew hot air at me. The rear windshield wiper was frozen pointing upward. The rear lock now only worked if I turned it with the key. A crack had finally finished its slow journey across the bottom of the windshield, and the molding was missing from the entire right side of the windshield glass, having ripped off on a windy day crossing Nebraska the week after Tess and I had started dating almost three years prior. A low rattle came from the gearshift, but if I turned the music up enough, it disappeared.

I could have afforded a much better car, I thought, battling traffic on the freeway out of Denver on July 30th. Oh, somebody just please let me get the hell out of here and get to Wyoming tonight. But I also could have afforded a nice house and some nice furniture. Would I be happier right now in a new car, stuck in traffic with my broken heart? My girlfriend would have still left me, no matter what I was driving or what kind of house I lived in. What was I doing?

You know what's nice about this car, I said to myself. My coffee mug fits in the cup holder. And this thing, for five years, has run on my belief in it. It's broken down once. One time in five years. And I still believe in it, even though I don't know shit about cars or engines. Baki believes in my car, too. Maybe that and a gallon of gasoline for every 25 miles is all we need for this.

--

At the end of five miles of Redfish Lake, the insurmountable-looking porcupine top of the Grand Mogul stands like a fortress on one side of the water, and its sibling, Mount Heyburn, sits on the other side, holding guard over the deep alpine valley bisected by Redfish Lake Creek. The two peaks are the east end of the Sawtooth Range. To get back into the mountains to climb, you can walk the five miles of trail around the lake or you can take a boat taxi, which is what you do if you want to add an air of adventure to your trip. Give the guy at the dock $8, chuck your 40-pound backpack into the front of the boat, and watch the pine-tree-lined slopes on the side of the lake pass by at 20 mph as you bounce over the waves in the water with the wind on your face.

On the southwest end of the lake, I bent over the dock and heaved my backpack out of the front of the boat. A 40-pound backpack never gets any more pleasant to carry, and it had been a while since I'd done it. Brian and I had spent an hour in the Redfish Lake Resort parking lot packing everything we needed for our trip into the Sawtooths: A 4-pound tent, sleeping bags, pads, pots, pans, fuel, two days of breakfast, two days of dinner, two days of snacks, and climbing gear, including two ropes weighing a total of 17 pounds, a full rack of cams, chocks and carabiners.

We plodded up the trail toward Alpine Lake. My hips hurt, my spine gently compacting under the weight of my pack. Just have to get used to it again, I told myself. I knew the waist belt of this six-year-old pack would break blood vessels in the skin covering my hip bones, the part on a man where there's no fat, and it would leave marks on my skin. After two or three days of walking with the pack on, though, I'd be broken in again.

Everything in me was familiar with the pain, and my legs knew the pace they could handle without bursting my heart. My feet hurt, but knew they could take it, even though it had been a long time. We walked through the trees along the contour of Redfish Lake Creek, steadily creeping uphill as the creek flowed downhill opposite us. The trees opened every few feet to reveal the steep canyon walls that topped out in jagged spires of granite. If there were a road to this trailhead, the Sawtooths would be a national park.

There are all kinds of hell you can put yourself through in the outdoors, but mountaineering is my favorite for its slow suffering. A long day with a heavy backpack is usually just the beginning.

Some people remember watching certain pivotal football games with their friends, remember who they were with when the Red Sox won the World Series; or they remember events in each others' family lives, show up for each others' dance recitals, flag football games and christenings. The mountains are where I remember being with my friends. The timeline of any friendship is a series of scenes or memories, times when you were together over the course of the relationship. I've spent plenty of time with my friends drinking coffee and sharing dinner at restaurants; but those scenes always fade into the background, overshadowed by adventures like this. Brian and I, just that year, had gone rock climbing in Boulder Canyon near Denver in January, in the snow; we had done a long climb in the Flatirons on a short February day and I had fallen on the descent, nearly crushing myself with a boulder the size of a microwave. We had spent Thanksgiving together the year before in Canyonlands National Park in the red-rock Utah desert.

With Brian living in Wyoming for the summer, an Internet photo of an Idaho peak called Warbonnet caught our attention. Warbonnet, a granite finger pointing up into the sky, requires six pitches of roped climbing, and has sheer drop-offs at the summit. After topping out, it takes three 200-foot rappels to get off the mountain. And it's miles from the trailhead, in wilderness, making the idea of a rescue distant in one's mind as the tasks become more dangerous.

Accountability is high even when climbing is not difficult — Warbonnet's South Face route is a moderate 5.7, but thoughts of loose rock, rockfall, exposure to weather and finding the correct line to the summit were enough to keep me from sleeping too peacefully in the nights leading up to our climb.

A stuck rope high in the mountains can lead to nerve-wracking delays, expensive gear left behind for rappelling, and exposure to lightning, rain, and snow, which can lead to hypothermia and all kinds of stuff that can happen when you're out with no shelter. Maybe what I loved about it was the potential that one thing going completely wrong could put us in a situation where we had no excuses, nowhere to point fingers. Besides geology, there isn't much out of your hands as a climber. There are no other players to blame things on, no coaches, no bosses, no coworkers, no politics, no bullshit. You either make it to the top or you don't. You either survive or you don't.

At the trail junction to Alpine Lake, close to the halfway point of our hike in, a young couple with big packs, ropes, and helmets said they had heard from a guide that the pass to Warbonnet was still covered with tons of snow. The guide had told them there was no way of getting up and over it without an ice axe. On a steep snow slope, a fall usually means sliding until something stops you, which can sometimes be a pile of rocks, which is never good. People have fallen while walking across relatively easy terrain, slid, picked up speed, smashed into boulders, and died from internal injuries within minutes.

Shit. I had two ice axes in the car, one for each of us, an hour-and-a-half hike back, and a boat ride across the lake. It was already 2 p.m. If we went back, it would be dark by the time we got up to the pass.

Well, we'll head up there and see what we think, I said to the couple. Maybe this will just turn into a backpacking trip. In my head, I was cursing myself. Why the hell didn't I bring those ice axes? It was what, another two pounds on this already monstrous pack?

At Alpine Lake, we looked at the slopes above that led to the ridge we had to cross. Snow choked every single couloir angling up to the spine of the mountain. This was not going to happen. Brian didn't want to give up, insisting that we could find another couloir to the left and get up and over. We spent three hours scrambling up granite slabs, across loose scree, snowfields, and finally up a dirty gully to the ridge.

We made it to the top of the ridge. But at the top, we saw we'd have to scramble across a half-mile of rock on the ridge to get back to where we were supposed to cross. We couldn't see the Bead Lakes, where we planned to camp at the base of our climbing route. It was on the other side of the ridge, probably a mile or more over blocky terrain that looked like it would require hands and feet to cross. No way were we going to attempt that scramble with an hour and a half of daylight left, not with 40-pound packs on our backs.

I'm sorry, I said to Brian. I have two ice axes in the car, what the fuck.

Hey, he said, it's August, the month of the year that everything, even up high, is supposed to be snow-free. Who would have thought we'd need ice axes? Let's go down, camp at the lake, and drive to City of Rocks tomorrow.

The City meant rock climbing right from the car, no heavy packs to haul ten miles, no snow to get in our way. I had never been there, but it sounded nice.

City of Rocks is a national reserve in southern Idaho, somewhat famous for its hundreds of rock climbing routes, and potential for probably hundreds more on its unexplored and undeveloped granite faces. If you told someone it was on the way to anywhere, you'd be lying. It was in kind of a no-man's-land just north of the Utah border, hanging out above the part of Utah no one ever drives through. But Brian had a Greyhound ticket from Salt Lake City back to Green River, and I was due at a trade show in Salt Lake the day after his bus left.

We turned around to go back the way we had come, and the entire valley behind, our afternoon of hiking uphill under those heavy packs, opened up underneath us. We stood on a once-in-a-lifetime perch trying to take in the swell of spires and peaks to the northeast, dropping down into the Redfish Lake Creek valley, and the very end of Redfish Lake, way out there barely sneaking around the corner, where the boat had dropped us off that afternoon. It was the first time I'd ever stood there, in that spot, and it would be the last. I knew it without a second thought. It was a fool's errand battling our way up to the pass, and I would never come back, not even for the view. I snapped photos furiously as the light started to fade. No one I ever met would ever see this, except through my photo, and maybe no one would ever again stand here.

We sidestepped and scrambled down the slope, crossed several streams, and, a few minutes before dark, set up our tent beside Alpine Lake, where we battled the mosquitoes. As soon as we finished dinner, we hurried into the tent, zipping the doors shut and hoping no bugs had followed us in.

I had talked to Brian all day, and we'd had everything else to worry about — the climb, the weather, the route, our safety, darkness. But the minute I zipped myself into my sleeping bag, I had no distractions. There was still a fresh wound. Thirty-one days before, I lay in our Denver apartment, already kept awake by the heat, lying on my side looking at her empty side of the bed, my hand extended out to where she would have been, and I knew it was never again going to be the way it was. If I thought to myself that night, "Maybe she'll come back," the "maybe" was so small you wouldn't be able to see it if the sentence were printed on a newspaper page, unless you were gazing through a magnifying glass.

I fidgeted around in my sleeping bag in the tent next to Alpine Lake. I just wanted peace, to not think about it for one night, to sleep tired sleep, like a little kid who wants to go to sleep not thinking about the monsters in his closet, knowing that if he starts to think about them, he won't stop.

--

Nobody really comes to see Ernest Hemingway's grave in the town of Ketchum — there's no special display, not even a sign on the highway pointing it out. He spent the last two years of his life in a house near Sun Valley, but the house isn't marked or really visited. The house where he lived in Key West is a museum, a venue for weddings, and home to 50 six-toed cats. Hemingway's grave in Ketchum is covered in coins, but no other fanfare. It doesn't have its own Web site. You just park at the cemetery and walk up to the grave with his name on it: Ernest Miller Hemingway, July 21, 1899 — July 2, 1961. It sits beside the grave of his last wife, Mary Welsh Hemingway. They both have full-length headstones, but his is the one that gets the coins, the wine bottle, the notes, and the shotgun shell someone left.

I'd already been there once, standing in front of his headstone, eight years before. I didn't need to stop there again, but it felt like something I should do on a road trip — this is what road trips are made of, right? The random stops on the side of the road, places that are special for one reason or another, even if they're not special to everyone? Brian and I pulled off the road and started walking toward where I thought it was, under a certain tree, near the middle.

I didn't pray or try to have a moment of silence or anything that you're probably supposed to do when you're standing above the dead body of someone buried in a wooden box. What are you supposed to do? It's Ernest Hemingway. Surely our visit was more meaningful than getting married at his house in Key West, right?

I held Hemingway up as one of the masters of writing. He didn't fuck around with a bunch of flashy, flowery writing, didn't waste words. With only the right details and nothing more, he painted a picture and told the story that needed to be told. That was it. No bullshit.

Nine years before I stood in front of his grave with Brian, I had read *The Old Man and the Sea*, a few months before I went to graduate school to learn how to be a journalist. I sat on the front stoop of my house in Cedar Falls, Iowa, smoking cigarettes, drinking coffee, reading by the porch light on a summer night. Nobel Prize. It was as good as they always said. I was enthralled. I started to pick up worn paperback copies of his other books in thrift stores—*For Whom the Bell Tolls*, *A Farewell to Arms*, *The Sun Also Rises*.

They were classics, something to emulate, if I could figure out how, without copying him.

A few months into my graduate studies at the University of Montana, I found an article in the October 1994 *American Journalism Review*, in which Ron Javers, a journalism professor at Syracuse University, laments the fact that none of his students read anything more intelligent than *Cosmopolitan*, and wonders how they'll ever learn to become great writers if they never read. The piece is called, "Where Are Today's Hemingways?" Javers writes:

> *Nobody ever taught Hemingway to write like Hemingway. He taught himself. And books were the tools he used.*

> *Real books, not textbooks. Most of the writing textbooks I've seen are flaccid collections of tired formulae, faux-wit and received wisdom. There are doubtless exceptions. But even great textbooks cannot help us solve the problem that confronts lovers and teachers of writing. Many students don't read: Not for pleasure, at any rate.*

> *Like many other writers before him and since, Hemingway was a voracious reader. He read writers like Shakespeare and Milton and Donne. And he read the work of contemporaries like Gertrude Stein, Ezra Pound, F. Scott Fitzgerald and Sherwood Anderson.*

Back in grad school, I knew I wanted to write, to be a writer. What, I wasn't sure. I had read books — the great books — my entire life. Shouldn't I be ready? Hemingway, Kurt Vonnegut, F. Scott Fitzgerald, Hunter S. Thompson, George Orwell, Edgar Allan Poe, Kerouac, Tolstoy, Dostoevsky, Gabriel Garcia Marquez, Kafka, John Steinbeck, Wallace Stegner. No one assigned me books to read; I just read them.

If any of that reading was training me, just like Hemingway trained himself 80-some years ago, the stuff that came out of my keyboard should be pure gold, shouldn't it? If it wasn't, there was no hope.

After journalism school, I had lived by writing the lede for stories. I strove for one sentence that could hook you, could pull you in and get you started on a story. The rest would follow. I said lines like "I don't believe in writer's block," borrowed from *Wonder Boys*, and would tell people, "You know what Hemingway said? He said 'Write one true thing.'"

He didn't say it, he wrote it, in A Moveable Feast, one of his books I hadn't read:

Sometimes when I was starting a new story and I could not get it going, I would sit in front of the fire and squeeze the peel of the little oranges into the edge of the flame and watch the sputter of blue that they made. I would stand and look out over the roofs of Paris and think, "Do not worry. You have always written before and you will write now. All you have to do is write one true sentence. Write the

Hemingway was a man's man, a hunter, a fisherman, and he said things like, "Only bullfighting, mountain climbing and auto racing are sports. The rest are merely games." He drank heavily. He drew on experiences from war, the theatre of masculine aggression, for his stories.

What was I going to write about? I didn't know how to hunt, didn't really want to, couldn't drink anymore, and didn't fish. After I left Montana, I discovered rock climbing and mountaineering. Climbing was adventurous, dangerous, exciting, romantic, and gave me grist for years of stories. Except I wasn't stoic like Hemingway. Climbing scared the shit out of me. But I kept going back. It gave me a reason to drive all over the West, exploring new places to climb in Utah, Arizona, Colorado and Wyoming. Places to give me pictures to paint in my stories, a narrative to pin my thoughts onto.

For three years, I had tried to sell a book manuscript to dozens of publishers and literary agents, with no luck. The book was about how climbing saved my life after I finished rehab, and gave me direction, an identity. I had sent off dozens of query letters and e-mails, and gotten dozens of rejection letters in return. I got a few bites, a few who were really interested, who even read the whole manuscript and not just a sample chapter. They'd give me hope, but in the end said things like "I'm just not completely in love with your writing voice" or, "We just don't know if we can sell this."

So here I was, eight years out of grad school, a few national magazine articles with my name on them, but no book, no great work to hold up, to point to and say, "I'm an author." Hours of sweating over notebooks and computers in coffee shops, opening up and putting my soul into 50,000 words, and nothing. Yet. Was I a writer?

Maybe I wanted to ask Hemingway that, through that headstone and six feet of dirt and the top of his coffin. Or maybe somewhere in my head thought standing there would help.

Shouldn't we all have a place like that in our lives? A place we make a pilgrimage to that means something special to us but maybe no one else we know? Something out there, at the end of a long drive, that we go see once?

--

Brian and I arrived in City of Rocks in a downpour at the end of 20 miles of dirt road. Two hours after parking the car, the rock was dry, and I was halfway up a route in the middle of a 90-foot wall of granite, hanging onto sticky handholds and stemming my legs out at 45-degree angles on opposite walls, my sticky-soled shoes holding me in the corner. A friend had described climbing at the City as "crack-protected face climbing," meaning you don't have to use crack techniques—wedging your hands, fists, fingers, toes, and feet into the gaps in the rock to pull yourself upward—to climb there. Brian and I would manage 14 pitches of climbing in less than 48 hours at City of Rocks, motivated but certainly not overachieving.

As American rock climbing goes, City of Rocks is one of the more middle-of-nowhere places to go. The nearest flush toilet is in Almo, Idaho, a town of about 100 people five miles to the east from the middle of the City. On our drive in from Burley, Idaho, we had sat in the car off to the side of the dirt road while a couple cowboys led several dozen head of cattle right down the road, the cows passing beside the Subaru as if it were broken down in the middle of a freeway. I wondered if one of them would knock my side mirror off and not even notice. The cowboys didn't make eye contact or even look at the car as they rode by on their horses, and, for a second, maybe it felt like the West was still a little wild.

A dirt road weaves through the middle of City of Rocks, passing granite monoliths and columns, giant grey noses of rock and elephant heads scattered every couple hundred feet, some 100 feet high, some 600 feet high. The rock is in places low-angle enough for children to scramble up, and in others steep enough to spit off strong climbers. The rock is made for climbing, the patina worn away into edges and holes in the rock that grab fingertips and toes of climbing shoes.

Places like this, where the climbing is so close to the road, often have signs that indicate that untrained or unprepared climbers should not scramble on the rock. Garden of the Gods, near Colorado Springs, draws the curiosity of many tourists, who start to climb up some of the formations in hiking shoes, then realize they've gotten themselves into a spot where they can't climb down, and either have to be rescued, or they sometimes accidentally fall. Devils Tower National Monument has similar signs warning people not to climb on the rock without proper safety equipment. Ever since I've climbed, I've found it to be a natural set of movements and remembered how much I liked to climb trees as a child. I never wonder why we have to put signs everywhere. The curiosity is so natural, whatever it is that makes us want to climb something, the pull is so strong to put your hands on the rock and start crawling up, that we have to remind ourselves that it's dangerous. Like the signs that say "no running" at a swimming pool, because kids are young, they're excited, they're having fun, and they forget the bad things that can happen to them because they haven't been suffocated by all the rules yet. They move concerned only with the maximum amount of fun they can have before it's time to go home.

At City of Rocks, I knew I was in the same emotional space as the summer I got divorced three years earlier, the summer I met Tess. I climbed with a tremendous appetite, taking anyone willing up any climb, just to get out and be on the rock. I would put myself on a route that pushed my limits, scared me, put me in a place where fear overwhelmed almost everything— most importantly the feelings of heartbreak and loneliness and the uncertainty of the future.

And here I was again, climbing.

I stood watching the light fade over the southern formations at the City as Brian cooked dinner on our last night there. I had never had the chance to spend a summer climbing, like so many people I knew—folks who had lived out of a van in Yosemite, spent an entire fall in Joshua Tree or Red Rocks. By the time I discovered climbing, I was already through graduate school, had no more summers off from college, and it was time to start making a living.

But there I was in the City for a few days, at the beginning of a month or longer away, and my fingertip pads had been worn down by the granite, my hands and ankle bones dinged with a few small cuts, and my pants were coated in chalk dust and dirt. I was getting that chance, at 32. I felt lucky to still be making a young man's memories, standing in the middle of this paradise of granite in the middle of nowhere with a friend, tilting at windmills, outside in the good air, playing, doing something simple. I closed my eyes for a second, inhaled deep, and smiled a little.

THREE

After his sink bath at the Flying J truck plaza in Snowville, Utah, Brian said, "I want to know what this 'Showers are for professional drivers only' policy is. What exactly is a 'professional driver'?"

"I don't know," I said. "I'd like to think I'm a pretty good driver. Like can Jeff Gordon shower there?"

"I would imagine that he could," Brian said. I-15 felt hot and fast and dusty after the 30-mile dirt-road drive from our quiet campsite at City of Rocks. Cars whipped by at 75 mph past the golden mountainsides baking in the midday sun. We moved south, easing into the 100-plus-mile stretch of suburban development that begins in Brigham City and extends all the way to Spanish Fork, with Salt Lake City in between.

I dropped Brian off at the Greyhound station early in the evening and met some friends for dinner. Thousands of people were in town for the

Outdoor Retailer trade show, the largest gathering of outdoor sports retailers, manufacturers, and media representatives in the country, a hotbed of opportunity for a freelance writer like me. After Tess left, I decided at the last minute to attend. I felt calm, pulling into town after five days of being in the outdoors. I smelled bad, but I felt good.

--

Rock climbing without a rope is only stupid and selfish if you slip and fall and die, which is something you think about every few seconds when you look down and see a couple hundred feet of air beneath your feet.

Part of me agreed to climb the West Slabs of Mount Superior with Chris without a rope just because all the guys at the company where he worked did it without a rope. They would start at 5 a.m. on weekdays, hike up the gully with an ice axe, put on rock shoes at the base, scamper up the 1,000-foot face in about a half-hour, scramble down the back in an hour or so, and drive to the office by 9 a.m.

The other part of me knew that I only did shit like that when my heart was broken, when no one was at home worried about me. If Tess knew I was out doing something like that, something reckless, she wouldn't speak to me for two days, and then we'd fight about it for days afterward. She would scold me like a little kid who knows better than that, and I would deserve it. Everyone's got different reasons for climbing ropeless, and different comfort zones.

How did I feel about it? As long as I was concentrating, keeping three points of contact on the rock, staying focused, not making any dumb mistakes, I thought my odds were OK, maybe even relatively good.

But that's not what I was doing up there with Chris. I was just going fast, distracted, getting sloppy. Getting ready to make a really stupid mistake. Most of the rock is solid, not going to break off in your hands, and it saw enough traffic that any loose blocks had been pulled off by previous parties. But parts of it were a little loose, fragile, not to be trusted.

It wasn't nearly vertical, slanting at an easy angle for most of the way up. It was still hands-and-feet climbing, though in plenty of places you could stop and take both hands off the rock if your footholds were steady.

Concentrate, concentrate. It was easy, but not safe, I told myself. Then my foot popped, slid a little bit down the rock, my heart leaping just a little bit. Shit. I pulled hard on both hands and my other foot. Stop. Take a breath. No rush here.

Then part of me, just a little part, shrugged and said no one would give a fuck if I fell off this thing and ended up in 15 pieces in the talus 500 feet down there. I knew it wasn't true, which is what people would tell you if they heard you say something like that.

As we climbed higher, the east suburbs of Salt Lake spread out underneath us. Chris had pointed this climb out to me from the city at least half a dozen times. The 1,000-foot-tall piece of rock was pretty easy to spot, even from a thousand feet below it and a couple miles away.

--

Chris was 29, married a couple years to Natalie, and he'd been having a career crisis since I met him three years before, but it seemed to have calmed. Natalie was driven, knew what she wanted to do professionally, and was successful at her development job for the International Rescue Committee.

After noticing each other around the Colorado State University campus a few times during their sophomore year in college, Chris and Natalie had met while working together at a vegetarian restaurant in Fort Collins. Chris was a dishwasher and Natalie was a hostess, until they started doing catering work together and Natalie became his boss. He still playfully called her "Boss Lady" over the phone and in person, when they discussed weekend plans or where they wanted to go out for dinner.

"I'm getting chickens or kids," Natalie said to Chris one night as we sat at the dinner table, smiling and only half-joking. Salt Lake, like many cities, had begun to allow city residents to keep chickens in their yards. Natalie wanted fresh eggs, straight from the chickens in their backyard in southeast Salt Lake City.

I asked Chris about it later. "It's actually 'kid,' not 'kids,'" he said. "The issue is whether we want to have one or not."

Tell me about it, I thought. One child was the same as four, to me.

Still, I had always assumed Chris and Natalie had agreed on it before they got married two years earlier.

They owned a house together in Denver, where I met them when Chris and I worked together. They left for Salt Lake City when Chris got an entry-level job with a ski and climbing equipment company he'd always wanted to work for, and Natalie landed a job with the International Rescue Committee. I missed them in Denver, but they seemed really happy in Salt Lake. A little less culture, I thought, and the weather wasn't as great as Denver's, but the access to the mountains was unparalleled: skiing and climbing within 30 minutes of their house. Natalie liked to climb, liked to ski, but they were Chris's passions—whenever conversation turned to the mountains, he lit up and started talking talking talking. I always saw their move to SLC as a sacrifice Natalie made for Chris, farther away from her family in Denver and closer to Chris's career and outdoor pursuits. I wondered how much relationship currency that gave her in the chickens/kids realm.

"Well, you guys have a few years to talk about it," I said. I had lately started doing math when I thought about where my friends were in life compared to where I was, in regards to relationships and children: How much time did we all have before it was too late, sealing our own fate and guaranteeing that we would die old, alone, and lonely? Let's see, she's 29, so that gives them six years. Even if they want to have two children, they can start when they turn 31. Or, she's 33, so if they don't have kids pretty soon, maybe it's not going to happen. Chris and Natalie had all the time in the world, I thought. Hell, she could get the chickens, change her mind, and then decide she wanted kids instead, and still have three of them before she turned 35.

Where was I? Tess had said I wasn't excited *enough* about having children. I had been warming up to the idea since my divorce three years before, and I thought I would definitely be ready for it in the next two or three years, by the time Tess was 30 or 31. Plenty of time. I just needed to push past this point in my career. Things were happening for me, and I needed lots of time, lots of long days during the week, to keep the ball moving forward. But in two or three years? I'd be able to say no to projects. The momentum would be with me, and maybe I could be a guy who wrote a few things and helped juggle a baby or two.

I had been trying to learn to be a fun uncle with my niece and nephew and Tess's nephew. I was still not much for holding newborn babies, but I had started to get comfortable, to have fun around 2-year-olds. Kids weren't so bad. It was fun for me to see the world through a 2-year-old's eyes, just like everybody says it is.

I liked the idea of having my kids home when they were in college or adults, and watching them grow into the incredible people I thought they'd be, and teaching my son or daughter to climb with me or just taking them to movies or whatever. Settle down and have some babies? Maybe. But right now, I had to work on my writing. I mean, how excited did I need to be about having kids? I felt like I was more open to the idea than Chris was. And Natalie hadn't left him.

--

My friend Sara and I grabbed a cup of coffee outside the Salt Palace, had a seat on a bench. She got divorced the same year I did, was a writer and social media expert, and knew everyone in the outdoor industry. We had spent a lot of time discussing relationships in the past, and she would counter my "because men are dumb" statements with cerebral things like, "Men aren't dumb, they're just simple creatures. They have simpler motivations than women."

I felt like I was just unloading on Sara, talking about Tess, what happened, what's next, why now, what am I going to do. I said, Look at me, I'm 32, and a younger woman just left me. I have a few grey hairs poking out here and here and here; I have wrinkles on my face, smile lines, forehead lines. Not a good time to be single, I said.

Oh, no, Sara said. Crow's feet are the best part of a man.

Shut up, I said. No one thinks that. And if you say you do, you're lying.

Oh, it's true, she said. I know plenty of women who will back me up on that.

And I saw a glimmer of hope.

--

I re-packed my car in front of Chris and Natalie's house in southeast Salt Lake City, saying goodbye to four nights in the same bed, four days of showers and wearing clean clothes, and heading back to the mountains, six hours of driving away. Once I cleared the multi-lane freeways in the SLC metro area, I would coast on uncrowded roads all the way back to Redfish Lake in Idaho, back to the Sawtooths. I could relax in that way you can when the only things on your mind are holding the steering wheel close to the middle and keeping the car at a velocity close to the speed limit. I could *drive*.

In the six years I had lived in central Denver, I had only driven to work a handful of times. I rode a bicycle year-round, and when the weather made the streets absolutely un-ridable, I walked. I felt lucky to live in a metropolitan area of three million people and have the choice to not drive. I chose to live an eight-minute bike ride from where I worked, to put up with the minimalist apartments and close neighbors so I didn't have to give away any of my time to stop-and-go-traffic, gas, brake, gas, brake, during the week.

In 2007, the average American spent 46 minutes per day commuting to work, which adds up to almost 200 hours per year of sitting in a car going to and from work. Two weeks' vacation is 80 hours. Commuting is not fun, as studies have shown, and thusly a lot of our driving is not fun. If there's an accident on the freeway or any other sort of traffic, driving becomes stop-

and-go, constant stress, merging, hitting the brakes, trying to stay up to speed in a gelatinous mass of cars whose velocity changes every 10 seconds.

Why do we do it? We want a big house. We work in the middle of cities, but most of us can't afford to live in the middle of cities. Unless we want to live in cramped apartments, no yard, no space for our kids to play. So we leave the city to live, to get a house with a yard, a couple extra bedrooms. Real estate agents tell us to "drive till you qualify." So we do, until we find what we think is the most house for our money.

And then driving, 20 minutes, 30 minutes, 45 minutes, becomes a chore. We try to make it tolerable with cupholders, convenience foods we can eat while we drive, books on tape, drive time talk radio, music, podcasts, hands-free cell phones, so we can talk to friends or family while we're performing the task of driving to and from work. But we still hate it. Does anyone remember the idea of "the freedom of the open road"? Because it's out there. Just not where most of us live.

Did we give up freedom for property in the early 21st century? As our housing bubble proved, the American dream of owning a home became a prison for many of us, who found we were "stuck" with a house in a down market, underwater on a mortgage and unable to sell, now shackled by the most house for our money—if not worse, facing foreclosure.

Sure, I hadn't had much space in any of my Denver apartments and definitely no yard. I didn't make the conscious choice to not buy a house—I had just never saved enough money for a down payment, never seemed to make the right decisions that would lead me to the place where a mortgage seemed like the next logical step in life. But I felt lucky, in our economy, to be able to walk away from a house and move into a car for a while, and just drive.

--

I drove north from Salt Lake City through Ogden and then Brigham City, exiting I-15 to head northwest on I-84 into Idaho as the sun poured out a warm mural of orange and yellow on the sky to the west. I draped a pair of running shorts over the steering wheel so the hot breeze would dry them in a few minutes.

I had draped all my cotton t-shirts and pants over the seats and spread all the gear in the seats, so it would dry. I didn't have enough time to throw the clothes in the dryer at Chris and Natalie's house before I left SLC. The next day was Monday, and I wasn't going to an office. I was going to sleep in my car on the way to Ketchum, Idaho, wake up in the morning, get groceries and pack a backpack for three days back up in the Sawtooths. Then I would shut my phone off.

At a pullout off the highway near Hailey, Idaho, I scrambled to rearrange all the backpacks and containers to make room to sleep in the back of the car. It was 11 p.m., and I needed to be up early to get to Redfish Lake. I wasn't going to waste a bunch of time driving 20 miles off the highway to find a campground and set up a tent so I could sleep in it for six hours.

If I pushed the front passenger seat forward a bit, I had just enough room to lie straight out, my feet against the rear hatchback door. I shoveled everything to the driver's side of the car, piling it against the windows, tossing a couple backpacks into the passenger seat. I rolled out a camping sleeping pad, my sleeping bag on top of it, brushed my teeth on the shoulder of the road, locked all the doors except the rear passenger side, where I got in the car and lay down. I locked the last door from the inside, tucked into my sleeping bag, and closed my eyes.

In the history of climbing culture, the term "dirtbag" has been transformed from pejorative to a term of endearment, almost to describe someone enlightened. A dirtbag is someone who lives simply, sometimes on small acts of charity from others, in order to focus on what matters to them: the pursuit of climbing, which, at some point in every climber's life, is close to holy. Climbers have lived off half-eaten slices of pizza in the cafeterias in Yosemite Valley, lived in tents for entire summers, even eaten cat food. In general, dirtbags live by thrift—preferring free campsites, legal or not, free food and coffee, cheap beer, and working as little as possible to make more time for climbing.

Sleeping in your car, if you're not a climber, might be seen as sad. If you're a climber, it's cool. It's thrifty without being trashy. Sleeping in your car in Indianapolis? Sad. Sleeping in your car on the way to climb the sandstone cracks at Indian Creek, Utah? Cool. Or that's what I told myself.

The American road trip culture was not one built on staying in a Marriott every night. Kerouac hitchhiked, stayed in friends' apartments, borrowed money, and was broke most of the time. Steinbeck, while very successful at the time he wrote *Travels With Charley*, slept in his car, although it was a custom-designed camper truck, which he named "Rocinante," after Don Quixote's horse. William Least Heat Moon took off on his literary journey for *Blue Highways* in a van equipped with a stove and a portable toilet. He named it "Ghost Dancing," and it now sits in the Museum of Anthropology at the University of Missouri. Chris McCandless, probably America's most modern-day road trip character, featured in the true story *Into the Wild*, lived truly minimally, donating his life savings to OXFAM before he left, then burning the last of his cash and leaving his car in the Arizona desert.

Keeping yourself clean, comfortable, and close to a refrigerator every night, in a warm bed—that wasn't part of the mythology of the road, and it sure couldn't be the way to any sort of enlightenment or healing, could it? I didn't want to be anywhere that would make me wish that Tess was with me, including a bed big enough for two people.

Still, I could have used a car with at least a completely flat surface to sleep on. The rear seat in the Subaru, when folded down, still angled up somewhat, like a hospital bed, and I slid toward the hatchback door all night.

FOUR

I bounced in my seat as the boat hopped the wake on Redfish Lake, on the same $8 boat ride Brian and I had taken after our failed climb in the Sawtooths a week earlier. I was back with my friend Teresa with two other summits on our list. The view of the mountains was no less spectacular and no less intimidating.

Teresa and I had become fast friends after meeting seven months before. She was born and raised in Seattle, a climber, skier, traveler, and writer, and worked for an outdoor apparel company. She was funny, sarcastic, and my friend Sara had told me that Teresa was the female me, as far as our writing was concerned. She happened to be in Idaho that week, planning to spend a few days at her parents' house in Ketchum, and we made plans to climb something. Didn't really matter what.

Teresa, 33, was dating but not finding anything close to perfect lately.

She communicates in anecdotes, like me, and we never run out of things to talk about—women, men, relationships, writing, climbing, food, music, being alone right in the middle of life when you're supposed to be settled down. When I had suggested climbing in the Sawtooths, she had been excited to get up and into the mountains she'd been looking at since she was young and visiting Ketchum with her family.

On my return trip to the trail at the end of Redfish Lake, I packed less climbing gear—no second rope, fewer cams and carabiners—going lighter, but not dangerously lighter. As we plodded back up the trail to Alpine Lake, I told Teresa about the book manuscript I'd been pitching to publishers and literary agents for the past few years.

"How many times has your book been rejected?" she asked.

"Probably fifty," I said.

All my life, I had listened to great songs and read great books and watched great movies, and some of them moved me to the point of tears welling up, chills, the hair on the back of my neck standing up, some sort of physiological reaction to incredible, created beauty. Some song by some band or a section of dialogue in a movie, a passage of writing in a book would resonate with me so deeply that I would think for just a second that maybe it was about me, about all of us. And all I wanted to do in my life was make one thing, one piece of art, a book, that did that for someone. Maybe for everyone.

All day, Teresa and I talked about relationships, life, and writing, and her different, non-male perspective on everything was refreshing. But when we were in the tent at night and when I woke up in the morning, I remembered there was a woman in the other sleeping bag six inches away from me, and it was my friend Teresa and not Tess. For a few seconds, I missed Tess, for the nights and mornings we had sleeping next to each other under the stars, waiting for the sun to wake us up. For what we had for a while when I thought it was good. For two and a half years, Tess had been lying next to me, a woman to climb with, someone else in the tent I could reach over and hug in the morning, somebody to take care of, to make sure she was warm enough every night. That was gone, and it hurt a little bit.

So the relationship hadn't been perfect. And maybe it wasn't right or even good for either me or Tess. And I couldn't go back. Was it OK that I missed it, and missed her? Was I going to have to do everything we did together again by myself, just to forget all the good times we had?

I have misjudged or miscalculated something very badly here, I thought, panicking a little. Two hundred and some feet up a rock chimney on the west face of Mount Heyburn, I couldn't see the ledge that was supposed to be at the top of the route, and I had only one more piece of gear I could place to protect myself from a fall. All the way up the route, I had placed a chock or a cam every 25 feet, meaning that if I fell before I placed the next one, I would fall more than 50 feet before the rope would catch me. If I hit anything on the way down when I fell, I would be in serious trouble.

Mount Heyburn is one of dozens of 10,000-foot peaks in the Sawtooths, and one of the most visible. From below, it was one of the meaner looking peaks I had ever tried to climb, a jagged mess of steep granite and snow-filled couloirs. Every route on it is Class 5, which means roped climbing for anyone who wants to try to stand on top of the true summit, which was only big enough for one person. It was like standing on something with the surface area of your typical living room end table, but with 1,200 feet of air beneath you in all directions.

Most of the way up the Stur Chimney, all I could think was how long it had taken us to get to the base of the climb, to where we got out the rope and started up: four hours of brisk hiking, scrambling over loose boulders, crossing a snowfield, and battling up two 35-degree fields of ball-bearing scree. And we had started that morning at our tent, which was probably at least two hours from a trailhead, back near the dock for the boat we had taken across Redfish Lake.

If I came off the wall, if my hand slipped off a hold or my foot broke off a rock knob I stood on, and I took that 50-foot fall and anything went wrong — my ankle caught a ledge on the way down, a rock dislodged from above and hit me in the head — it would take someone a long, long time to get there to help me. Teresa would have to walk all that distance down to the trailhead to get someone to help; a rescue would have to be organized and then begun. I'd be there overnight at the very least. If I didn't bleed out.

"Ten feet!" Teresa yelled from far below. I had ten feet of rope left between me and her. It was a 70-meter rope, which meant I'd climbed 220 feet without stopping. Yes, I had definitely misjudged something. I couldn't see the top. FUCK. I placed my last chock at about chest level and hoped I could find a ledge a few feet above to set up an anchor and belay Teresa, if I didn't run out of rope first.

Why was I out here on this mountain no one cared about, suffering through the hike to the base, dragging a rope and all this metal shit, just to climb one ropelength of rock and stand on top? I knew the answer, but it was the same panic question I always asked. Fuck me, what am I doing here? I could be doing anything in my spare time. Why am I risking everything for something so dumb? But I always knew why. This was what cleared my head, turned down the volume on every other thought I could have—Tess, my future, would I ever find someone else—all of that faded away as I concentrated fully on the next move, being safe, moving upward. Some people drink to forget about things for a while. Some people go shopping for new shoes. I climbed.

I pulled up on the next two handholds, and there it was: a giant boulder with a strip of nylon webbing around it. The angle eased off above, and that was the top of the roped climbing. We could scramble to the top from just above the boulder. I clipped myself to the webbing, ran another piece of cord around the boulder, and clipped into that. No rope to spare. I yelled down to Teresa that I was off belay and exhaled. And then I turned around and looked over my shoulder.

For 230 feet, I had climbed up inside three walls, my face pointed toward the back wall, scanning the inside of the chimney for handholds and footholds. Incrementally, I worked my way up, ignorant of the view that kept getting better and better behind me as I slowly rose. And now, LOOK.

Granite spires and jagged peaks went for miles out to the west, snow hanging on the north faces and couloirs, impenetrable terrain, mountains too fierce and angry to traverse. There are two ways you can see this view: from a plane or from one end of a climbing rope. And no one—or relatively no one—climbed in the Sawtooths. We'd seen other climbers on our hike in, but it was no Yosemite. Everyone was down on the proudest granite face in Idaho, the Elephant's Perch, not up on Mount Heyburn like we were, suffering for hours to get to a short rock climb. If we had sat on top of Mount Heyburn for two weeks, we'd be lucky to have six people visit us.

It was after noon and we needed to get down. In my head, I already was two-fisting ice cream cones at Redfish Lake Resort back at the trailhead. We stayed roped up, took turns belaying each other for the short traverse to the summit, no bigger than the roof of a sedan, across a 3-foot-wide catwalk with hundreds of feet of air on both sides. Almost six hours later, we plodded off the trail and back to our car.

--

From the town of Stanley, Idaho, the Sawtooth Range appears as regal as the Tetons. It's a mountain range that few Americans will ever see, because it's on the way to nothing else notable—unless, say, you decide to drive from Twin Falls, Idaho to Missoula, Montana. But maybe it's so beautiful because it's in the middle of nowhere. There's no interstate running in front of it, just two-lane State Highway 75 and the Salmon River coming off the pass at Galena Summit and calmly strolling north to the town of Salmon 150 miles away.

I drove north on 75 and then U.S. 93 toward Missoula, where I'd spent two years as a graduate student at the University of Montana eight years before. Before Tess, before my marriage and divorce. I hadn't been back to Missoula since.

Ocean waves of pine trees dropped hundreds of feet into the Salmon River, winding through the canyon, late morning sunlight dancing on the riffles as the water rolled over rocks in the wide spots of the riverbed. Willie Nelson gently, effortlessly laid out the verses of Paul Simon's "Graceland" on my car stereo with one speaker blown out in the back, and I sang along:

Losing love

is like a window within your heart

Everybody sees you're blown apart

I almost got all the words out before my off-key singing choked on a lump in my throat.

Tears blurred my vision; I blinked, holding my eyelids closed for a half-second, and the tears rolled out and down my face. It's OK, I said to myself. I'm a grown man, a mess, singing Willie Nelson and letting tears drop onto my shirt, steering my car down S-curves along this river; no one can see me crying as I fly down the road at 55 mph.

Men aren't supposed to cry, but fuck it, I had a broken heart, and that feels like cancer sometimes. You can tell everyone about it, and they can give you a hug, try to help you with some advice, but no one else can feel it, in your chest, where you have a brick tugging on it, pulling it down. You're alone with that feeling that maybe nobody besides your mother is ever going to love you, that you're going to die alone and that no one is ever going to get this gift of what you have inside you. And maybe all you want to do is share it with someone and make them laugh every day of their lives because it lights up your heart when they smile at you.

I was crying over my steering wheel in Idaho because of the hurt, because it felt unfair that I didn't have someone anymore; thousands of women are unhappy and wishing their boyfriends would pay more attention to them and less attention to a football game on TV, and all I wanted was someone to slow dance with me in my kitchen when "Beyond the Sea" came on the stereo. I got a heart this big, this big, you know, and no one to give it to. The day before, I was on top of a mountain, standing on a two-foot-wide piece of granite hundreds of feet above the Sawtooths, and today, I felt like I was back in high school wondering what's wrong with me that I don't have a date to the homecoming dance.

What's going to happen next? I wondered. I'm too old, too poor, and why do they always leave me and say that nothing was really that wrong? Goddammit. I flipped my sunglasses onto my forehead and wiped the tears down each cheek with the bottom of my open palm.

A friend said something to me about falling down and skinning your knee when you're a kid—you fall down and scrape your knee, and it hurts, but you don't cry. If your mother comes running toward you, *then* you start crying.

Why am I crying driving through the mountains, listening to Willie, I said. Maybe I feel like nobody loves me, but this place does. Maybe I'm rolling down this canyon, watching two thousand pine trees whip by my windows for every song that plays on the stereo, and this whole scene, this sunlight bouncing off the water and the mountainsides dropping into the canyon, is my mother, running around the corner to give me a hug, to tell me it's going to be OK, that my broken heart is going to heal, just like my skinned knee did.

When Tess said it was over, I knew where to go to let my heart empty out: this place that can fill it up again and make it whole, so I can open it to someone else one day. Love still hasn't been forever in my life, but these mountains will be.

I tore around another corner on Highway 93, still following the Salmon, ignoring one of the many signs about a historical marker in a quarter-mile on the right. The historical marker appeared, and there was a grey-haired man reading it with his hands clasped behind his back, a car parked next to him with no one else in it. He was traveling by himself, like me, but had time to stop at the historical markers, unlike me. Did he have all the time in the world? That would be so lonely. I imagined his story: His wife had died a few years ago, after they'd only enjoyed a couple years of retirement together. Their children were grown with their own families and loved it when Grandma and Grandpa visited, and felt bad that he was living in that big house all by himself now. But he couldn't come live with them, obviously. They were spread out, one in California maybe, the other in Chicago, and the whole family hadn't managed to get together for the holidays since Grandma had died.

Was he at peace, enjoying time by himself? Or did he miss her terribly, a giant hole in his life without her around? Was it too quiet at home, so he hit the road to see the things he'd always wanted to see but hadn't had the time? Was it lonelier out here for him or at home in that big empty house where the kids had grown up? Were his wife's clothes still in her closet?

--

Up until the point he said it, I thought the border guard and I were just having kind of a de-briefing conversation, in which we talked about my ancient criminal record, a couple DUIs and an obstruction of justice charge, almost 10 years old. Just a couple of guys talking, albeit in an interrogation room just on the Canada side of the U.S.-Canada border north of Eastport, Idaho. I was explaining some things to him, Ha ha, you know, dumb stuff you do when you're in college, right? Then he said,

"That's what your FBI file says."

Oh. That sounded like Tommy and I might not make it to Banff that night.

It was news to me that the U.S. Federal Bureau of Investigation might have a file with my name on it. The border guard was friendly but firm, holding a printout that was apparently my FBI file. I mean, I had driven drunk a couple times right after college, gotten caught, paid my fines, spent a little over a week in jail, completed probation, rehab, everything. I hadn't had a drink for almost nine and a half years, nearly a third of my life. Was the FBI investigating every hapless dipshit college kid who got too drunk a few too many times? I hadn't bought a copy of *Mein Kampf,* Googled "How do I build a pipe bomb?", or even downloaded music illegally in the past eight years or so. I had to have one of the least interesting FBI files in the entire world. But.

"As you might know, Canada's laws pertaining to drunk driving are more strict than the U.S.'s," he said, across the table. "Our drug laws are sometimes more relaxed, but our drunk driving laws are more strict. In Canada, you can be sentenced to up to 10 years in prison for what's called 'impaired driving,' so when looking at U.S. drunk driving convictions, we go back 10 years."

"OK," I said. I started to wonder if this wasn't just a formality, if I would still be on my way to Banff in a few minutes.

"It says here you were on probation. Do you remember when your probation ended?"

"I guess when I paid off my fine — maybe May or June of 2003?" It was a lifetime ago. I had been married, divorced, lived in three different states, seven different apartments, and had six different jobs since then. Probation. That was a different person, a young man learning lessons the hard way. I had wrinkles now. I had started to find grey hairs.

"OK, so you paid a fine, and that ended your probation. Was there any jail time with that?"

"Yeah, I did a week in jail and went to rehab for six weeks, all as part of my sentence. I haven't had a drink in nine and a half years."

"Oh, you went to jail?" He asked, emphasis on the word "jail," like it was in italics as it came out of his mouth, as if I had just told him that I had murdered someone and buried the body in my backyard. I wanted to say, Sir, in the part of Iowa where I'm from, drunk driving arrests are a rite of passage.

If you haven't hit a deer with your car or racked up a DUI, you're in the minority. People in my hometown don't even act like you might have a drinking problem until you have three DUIs.

I was talking too much, I knew, even as more and more words came out of my mouth.

"Yeah, it was a week, that was the mandatory minimum," I said. "I'm actually going to the Banff Centre to do a residency and write about the whole process, to work on a book about being a recovering alcoholic." He didn't care about the Banff Centre or my book or who I was besides what was written on that paper in front of him. I could have told him I was going to Banff to start digging a hole to China with a soup spoon, or that I wanted to see the Canadian Rockies before I died of MS in a few weeks, or that I had a rattlesnake farm in northern Alberta, and he wouldn't have batted an eye.

He wasn't mean or stern, just matter-of-fact. "Unfortunately, you can't come into Canada," he said. "There's nothing I can do from here. You can apply for something called Criminal Rehabilitation with the Canadian consulate in Seattle, but that will likely take a couple weeks. Unfortunately, there's nothing we can do here at the border."

"Wow, I had no idea," I said. No fucking shit I had no idea.

I've been done with this, I wanted to say, for nine and a half years. I can barely remember what beer tastes like anymore, and you tell me I am still some sort of a menace, that I can't come into your country as a climber and a writer? Wow. I couldn't have been more surprised if he had turned into a dolphin right in his chair.

Criminal rehabilitation requires but is not limited to:

- A photocopy of each court judgment made against you which must clearly show the charge, the section of the law under which you were charged, the verdict and the sentence.

- A photocopy of the foreign laws under which you were charged or convicted.

- Any documents relating to sentence imposed, parole, probation or pardon; e.g. court records, judge's comments, probation or parole reports, certificate of rehabilitation from public officials or respected private citizens, etc.

- A criminal clearance from the police authorities in all countries where you have lived for six consecutive months or longer since reaching the age of 18.

- A state certificate for each state in which you have lived for six consecutive months or longer since reaching the age of 18 and a national FBI certificate.

I wanted to say, Thanks, Canada, I know I'm rehabilitated because every day for the last nine and a half years, I have spent my entire day not drinking beer and whiskey, something I would love to do, and something every other adult American and Canadian has the right to do. I don't need to prove anything to you. I have proven it to myself by having spent more of my life not drinking than I did drinking, by taking almost a third of my time on earth and not giving in to the voices in my head.

I felt like I had better chances of getting into Harvard Medical School than I did getting into Canada.

In *Travels With Charley*, Steinbeck writes, "Government can make you feel so small and mean that it takes some doing to build back a sense of self-importance." That was after he got turned around at the Canadian border because he didn't have immunization papers for Charley, his poodle. He was asked to come into the office, had a brief interrogation and was sent back to the U.S.

Ending our chat, the guard left through his door in the back of the room, and I opened the door on my side and walked back into the waiting room.

"I need to buy you a plane ticket," I said to Tommy, who was patiently sitting outside the interrogation room. I felt sick.

"What?"

"Yeah, I can't go into Canada," I said. "What the fuck."

"I wondered if something was up," he said. We walked out of the building, turned the car around, and drove back into the United States, stopping off at the checkpoint to officially be allowed back into the country.

I apologized over and over again. I didn't know what to say, having promised Tommy a week of climbing in Banff, dreaming about it myself, buying guidebooks, studying routes, packing everything we'd possibly need, including crampons and two ice axes—one for me, one for Tommy. I'd have to e-mail the Banff Centre and tell them I couldn't attend my writer's residency because I was, apparently, still a criminal.

Tommy didn't once say anything down, anything remotely negative, nothing about it being my fault. We had a week to go, to climb somewhere— the Tetons, the Cascades, Yosemite, City of Rocks, wherever.

Steinbeck also writes in the first few pages of *Travels With Charley*, "A journey is a person in itself; no two are alike. And all plans, safeguards, policing, and coercion are fruitless. We find that after years of struggle that we do not take a trip; a trip takes us."

So Tommy and I pulled over into the parking lot of the Safeway in Bonners Ferry, Idaho, got out our atlas, and talked it over. Tuolumne Meadows, the higher, eastern area of Yosemite National Park, was a mere 18 hours' drive away, and Tommy still had a connecting flight out of San Francisco, if he skipped the first leg of his airline ticket home from Calgary. It was 1,000 miles of driving through parts of five states in a hot, packed car. But what was this trip about, anyway?

We drove to a convenience store and bought two large coffees.

FIVE

My friend Tommy Riley does not seem like someone who spends his days working at a place like the Art Institute of Chicago. He has the name of a native New York City firefighter, and he talks like a fifties greaser sometimes. He works on his own car and has a thick black mustache fit for an auto-body-shop owner. Judging by his appearance, you'd assume he drives a Camaro, drinks Budweiser and listens to Billy Squier; but his taste in music is current, and good—hip, even. He loves to tell people about randomly seeing classical violinist/art-rocker Andrew Bird around town. But he still says things like "kid sister," occasionally refers to women as "chicks" or "broads," and every once in a while lapses into language like he's been hanging out on the set of *Happy Days*. His extended family members all play instruments, and when they get together, they play Jim Croce songs. Tommy sometimes sits in on the drums when someone needs a break.

I like Tommy because I think he is everything that is good about the working class in American cities (or used to be), even though he has a white-collar job. He was born and raised in the south Chicago suburbs, loves the city, loves the White Sox, and hates the Cubs. He will tell you that a garage, on the south side of Chicago, is known as "The Party Room." I like a guy who still believes in drinking beer in a garage. Tommy does whatever the fuck he wants for fun and doesn't care if it's cool or not, and, whether or not you think whatever it is is cool, you want to go do it with him, because he's so earnestly excited about it—sweetly. After growing up going to punk shows, he was now 32 and into honky-tonking.

Twelve hours into our 18-hour drive from Eastport, Idaho to Lee Vining, California, Tommy looked over at me and said, "You ever think about switching the driver's seat with the passenger seat in this thing?"

"No, why?"

"Well, in theory, it's got about half as many miles on it," he said. "You think about it, the only thing wrong if you switch them is the recline handle is on the inside. It still works."

"Wow," I said. A few weeks before our trip, Tommy had repaired a hole in the exhaust on his 1992 Ford Explorer using a Miller High Life can to replace a rusted-out section of pipe. I had seen photos. Tommy believed in keeping vehicles alive as long as possible, as opposed to the American tendency to buy a new car as soon as one got a little old, dirty, or near

100,000 miles. He called himself a "shade tree mechanic" or a "ghetto mechanic," and would every once in a while in conversation enthusiastically say brilliant things like, "Man, getting a new windshield is like getting a new car!" And then I started to wonder what it would be like if I replaced my windshield and didn't have to squint through a million tiny dings every time the sun was low in the sky. Maybe it was worth the $200 to get a new windshield, if Tommy said so.

If you were to get turned around at the Canadian border and your plan of climbing for a week in Banff completely disintegrated, Tommy Riley was the guy you wanted with you. I figured we could get to California in two days, if we could handle that much time in the car. It was 18 hours away, and we made it in 26 hours, stopping to sleep once in a cheap hotel in Connell, Washington.

We drove the entire north-south length of Oregon, 365 miles from the Washington border to the Nevada border, in the middle of a hot August day, over the golden hills and the empty plains and the desert mountain ranges, passing through only nine towns of a size large enough to support a convenience store. Sweat dripped down the fronts of our shirts, and we got out of the car at gas stations, damp everywhere, soaked front and back.

And that was just the start. We were numb already. Another two hours to Winnemucca, Nevada, as the sun sank. We stopped at a truck stop at the south end of town, where all the people there made me feel like we had just returned from the moon. We hadn't seen more than a handful of cars since Burns, Oregon, a dusty outpost four hours back, and I had silently worried that my spare tire wasn't inflated in the back of the car, and we would get a flat and spend the night out in the desert with no cell signal. It was a bigger kind of loneliness than I'd felt driving anywhere else in America.

Tommy Riley would not complain about the lack of air conditioning in a car on an 18-hour drive through the desert in the summertime. He wouldn't complain about anything, as my friend Nick had once told me. Nick and Tommy had been coworkers at Breckenridge Ski Resort in 2004, bumping lift chairs and sampling the ski-bum life for two years. Tommy said he and air conditioning had a contentious relationship, meaning he had never actually had it in any of his cars. So he was fine leaking sweat out of every pore on an endurance drive in my shitty Subaru, and excited about climbing in Yosemite.

We drove in the dark through Nevada, rabbits sprinting across the road just in front of the car every three or four minutes south of Hawthorne, Nevada. I wildly swerved to avoid them, the car's headlights sweeping both sides of the road, until I eventually hit one and hopefully killed it. Mostly I was too exhausted to feel that bad about it as its body thudded into the bottom of the cab as we rolled over it at 75 mph.

At 11 p.m., we crept into the Big Bend Campground a couple miles up the road from Lee Vining, California. I rolled out my sleeping bag, sure nothing would wake me, the soothing sound of Lee Vining Creek rolling by not far away.

I sat up the next morning at 7:30, feeling like we were somehow all of a sudden in California, at the eastern gateway of Yosemite, the most famous climbing area in the country.

Tommy had never climbed anything higher than a half-ropelength, or about 100 feet. The rock climbing outside Chicago doesn't tend to be very high. The first day in Tuolumne, we romped up an easy climb on Tenaya Peak—1,500 feet of low-angle granite to a summit that looked down on Half Dome and the Yosemite Valley to the West. Afterward, out of nowhere, Tommy asked me, "You know what I've been doing lately at work? Drinking out of a non-travel coffee mug. It's great. Makes you feel less rushed." And then we drove back to the campground, fist-pumping out the window to The Misfits' "I Turned Into A Martian."

--

I drove 30 minutes down Tioga Pass Road, dropping 2,400 vertical feet in 10 miles, zooming down the canyon to a roadside pullout just before the intersection with US 395, where I finally got cell service. As the sun dropped behind the mountains, Mono Lake started to fade into darkness, and I called Tess.

It had been almost seven weeks since we had said goodbye in front of the Denver airport, and that night and a few days after, she had e-mailed to say she wasn't sure. I had told her that I had no choice but to start trying to get over her once she got on that plane. I couldn't sit around and hope she would come back and have a change of heart.

She had spent a month working in Ecuador. No time to digest everything. While she was away, I sat in our home in Denver and disassembled our life together. Now she was back in the lonely apartment, and I was in Yosemite. We were on different timelines.

On the phone, looking over Mono Lake from the driver's seat, fiddling with the steering wheel with my other hand, I told her what I'd been thinking about: that she was right when she said she didn't know if we were right for each other; that maybe I had been trying so hard to make it work that I hadn't been able to admit that I wasn't happy; that I probably hadn't known that I wasn't happy until we had broken up.

Tess was back in Denver, boxing up the things that were hers, some of which had been ours seven weeks before: the bed, dishes, pots and pans, photos, the furniture. I knew how that felt—horrible, sad and lonely—and I felt bad that she was there alone. Even though we were broken up, I wished I could help her get through it. But I had done the same thing a few weeks earlier.

"You're my best friend," she said into the phone. "I don't want to lose you." I watched a car drive past, up the road on its way into Yosemite. She was crying, alone in our old apartment in Denver, maybe sitting on the floor between a couple of boxes, maybe looking at one of those photos of us. And I was here. I hated it.

I know, I thought. You're my best friend, too, and I lost you weeks ago.

Friendships for the most part die a natural, slow death. People get too busy for each other, move too far away, call each other less, and, one day, the only contact they have is an annual holiday card.

A breakup is a too-sudden, too-violent end to a friendship. Even when you can see it coming. The person you've shared everything with for so long, celebrated good news with, helped through bad news, is gone. The next good thing that happens to you, you will look at your phone and know you can't call the person who was your best friend a couple weeks ago. Maybe you'll call your mom. Bad news, you'll probably just deal with on your own for now.

I'm sorry, I said into the phone. I don't know what to tell you. This is part of it, the worst part. It hurts me, too; but it hurt worse four weeks ago, when I was moving out of the apartment and you were in Ecuador.

After an hour, we hung up. That was the last time I ever heard her voice. I started my car and started the climb back up Tioga Pass in the dark. Both my headlights had gone out. I wanted to pound on my steering wheel. Scream for ten minutes. Get out and kick something. Somehow let out the frustration. Why couldn't I just go back to Denver and put my stuff back in the apartment and be happy with Tess, propose to her with her mom's ring and have a happily-ever-after like everyone else?

But I knew it was wrong, and I had known it was wrong for a while, and I was so tired. and I just slouched over the steering wheel up the pass, staring out the windshield into the darkness all the way back to the campground.

--

This Is The Greatest Rock Climb I Have Ever Done, my hands and feet said to me on the granite knobs maybe a hundred feet below the summit of Cathedral Peak. I had danced up 600 feet of granite cracks and flakes all morning in the sun, not a cloud in the sky, Tommy following behind me.

The Southeast Buttress of Cathedral Peak is one of the most famous climbs in Yosemite, maybe California, maybe America. Search the Internet for information and you'll find descriptions with words like "best summit ever," "stupendous," and "spectacular."

It is 700 feet of easy, roped climbing, up immaculate granite, to a summit block that can accommodate only two or three people, a chair in the sky high above the domes and alpine valleys of Tuolumne.

Everyone loves it. It's like the Beatles. You can't experience it and act like it's not inherently good, or the best.

But it's also one of the most popular routes in the world, and it's usually crowded. As many as 40 people had been counted on the face on a fall

Saturday, making climbing slow, time-consuming and aggravating to many. Most of my climbing life, I'd tried to avoid crowded routes, for solitude and to allow myself an experience where I could get into my own head as much as possible, to avoid distractions, like other people climbing next to me and yelling to their partners and maybe kicking down rocks from above. Cathedral Peak was notorious for that type of scene.

But how could we not climb it?

For the first three days of our Yosemite visit, we had driven Tioga Pass Road through the Tuolumne Meadows area of the Park, seeing the domes: Fairview, Daff, Stately Pleasure Dome, pulling our eyes out the car window up and up until we craned our necks out to follow the titanic granite walls up to their rolling tops, moons that had dropped out of the sky and landed on the hillsides along the road.

At several stretches of the road, a pointed spike of clean, white granite would up on the horizon, in profile showing two summits, like someone made a mountain then bit off the top, leaving a round half-hole between the two peaks. All over this country, you can argue with names of mountains and rocks—this doesn't look like a sawtooth; that doesn't look like a flatiron or an elephant's head or whatever. But you can't argue with Cathedral Peak's name. It's one of the most beautiful mountains in America, otherworldly, a bizarre sculpture among natural forms. You don't wonder why John Muir wanted to climb it back in 1869.

On the quick drive to the trailhead at 5:30 that morning, I chugged 14 ounces of cold instant coffee and devoured two energy bars in two bites apiece, excited and nervous. We started up the trail just before light and saw no one. The approach meandered through the trees and over granite slabs, before battling up a loose slope to the base of the solid rock that swept up to the sky above us.

We racked up at the base, Tommy putting his pack inside mine and strapping it to his back for the climb. Easy, clean climbing at first gave way to slightly steeper pitches, comfortable but exposed, more and more air under our feet as we climbed higher, toward the point. On the fourth pitch, I crammed myself into a chimney, popped out the top and weaved all over the face trying to find the easiest route up. I built a belay and waited for Tommy. We hadn't seen another person all morning.

After a few minutes, a climber popped his head over a ledge below me. He climbed up to my anchor, no rope, no gear, just a chalk bag around his waist. He wasn't even wearing climbing shoes—he climbed in Merrell low-top hiking boots. I said hello; he said hello; I said Beautiful day isn't it, he said Yeah, right on, OK. Then he stepped onto a column just to the left of the cams and nuts securing me to the rock, and the column tipped, moving an inch toward me. If he pushed another 10 pounds of his weight onto his right foot, that block of granite, probably the size of a case of beer bottles, would rock off the ledge and bounce down 400 feet to the talus at the base of the climb. Maybe hitting Tommy on its way down. And if it hit Tommy, it would almost certainly kill him; and if it didn't kill him, it would definitely vaporize whatever extremity it did hit. You don't have to know anything about physics to know that a rock that big, falling 150 feet down, has enough speed behind it to destroy anything not made of what it's made of. My heart jumped.

"Whoa, better not step on that," the guy said.

"Yup," I said. And he climbed up and away. And that was it.

Twenty minutes later, I was climbing again, second-to-last pitch of climbing we would do, and the guidebook said my options were to go up a crack system or climb "5.7 unprotectable knobs." I picked the knobs. The knobs of Tuolumne were famous. If you chiseled hand- and footholds out of granite, those knobs are what you would make. They went on for 100 feet sometimes, a natural climbing wall, uncontrived, million-year-old stepladders that are granite's gift to the people who like to climb it. They sometimes ran out at bad times or were too far apart to be useful, and that could be scary. But the knobs on the fifth pitch of Cathedral Peak were pure bliss, the rock you didn't know you had wanted to climb your entire life, but when you did, you couldn't help but smile.

Up top, I told Tommy, Not bad, man. Not bad for a guy from Chicago who four days ago had never done a climb higher than 100 feet, never been on a multipitch rock climb. And there we were in Yosemite, the beating heart of American rock climbing, on top of one of its most famous climbs, the top of our twenty-third pitch in three days, taking in the view of the lakes and domes below from this perch at 10,911 feet.

Sometimes you have to sit in places like that for just a second and think about where you've been, where you came from, what other directions you could have gone as you were growing up, and take a deep breath. I could not have been happier that the border guard kicked us out of Canada.

--

America is a country where you can pull your car off the highway, fill up the tank with gas, and walk into a building where you can buy highly processed single-serving food, drinks, and possibly a wolf T-shirt, or a pleather NFL jacket, or a petrified alligator head. Or a 64-ounce refillable travel mug, a "The South Will Rise Again" bumper sticker, or a sleeveless western shirt. I like that.

Plenty of us spend our time seeking out great restaurants, telling each other about the risotto here, the lobster bisque there, the tomahawk steak, getting dressed up, dropping $150 on sushi for two, sampling the world's culture from our dinner tables, wiping our mouths with cloth napkins and signing the credit card slip for a single meal that will cost us four to six hours of work next week to pay off. I enjoy that stuff too.

But to me, the American convenience store is one of the best things about road travel in this country. Each store is a unique expression of local tastes, an effort to meet the needs and prey on the hunger and boredom of drivers and passengers, and an absolute desert of nutrition. Every time you pull off one of our great highways and into the parking lot of a convenience store, you find a different answer to the question, "Do you think anyone would buy this shit?"

Yes, we will, and I have. I will buy your donuts, your crusty roller-grill items, your crappy souvenirs, trashy clothing, miniature license plates with my friends' names on them, postcards from local attractions no one outside a 100-mile radius has heard of. If you have ugly sunglasses for $4.99, I am in the market.

I am a connoisseur of convenience stores. I have bicycled across the country, taking in a solid 2,000 calories a day from racks of cashews and potato chips, shelves of candy bars, and soda coolers. I have made feasts of plastic triangles stuffed with egg salad sandwiches, chocolate milk, and quarts of Gatorade while sitting on the curb watching drivers pump gas and heat bounce off the highway asphalt.

The Mobil in Lee Vining, sitting at the junction of the great American highway U.S. 395 and Tioga Pass Road, down the hill from Tuolumne Meadows, is the Mecca of American convenience stores. It is the Yankee Stadium among sports venues, and not just that, but a sold-out Yankee Stadium during Game 7 of the World Series. The best, the brightest, making every other place look like a dirt tee-ball field with no bleachers.

Just before our five days in Tuolumne Meadows, I sent text messages to some climber friends telling them where I was headed that week, and they all replied the same thing:

Go. To. The. Mobil.

We did. Too many times in the span of less than a week, maybe. I bought a T-shirt that said "The Mobil" on it. What is the best thing you've ever eaten at a convenience store? A passable slice of pizza? A donut that was actually cooked on the premises that day?

The menu at the Whoa Nellie Deli, in the back of The Mobil, includes: Herb Crusted Grilled Pork Tenderloin, St. Louis Style Baby Back Ribs, Lobster Taquitos, Wild Buffalo Meatloaf. The line goes 50 feet from the back of the store, out the front door, and spills out the sidewalk on weekdays at lunch time. How many gas stations have reviews like this on Yelp.com?

I wish the desserts weren't so expensive, but even at $7-$8 each, we still got the cheese cake and chocolate cake deserts and without alcohol I don't have any regrets paying $82 for lunch for two.

Three of us had the filet mignon that was the special. The filets were all center cuts and were prepared to perfection. It was paired with garlic mashed potatoes and a pile of fresh spaghetti squash. We topped the dinner off with a glass of the house Cab which was wonderful.

The Mobil took the convenience store and elevated it to the level of art, a piece of art that served incredible food and its own culture. I was completely blown away. I was standing above Macchu Picchu, a lifelong golfer hitting a straight drive down the fairway at Augusta, shaking hands with the President.

I heard The Mobil used to offer trapeze lessons not so long ago.

Our last afternoon in Tuolumne, Tommy and I were sitting on the curb in front of the Tuolumne Meadows store, finishing our afternoon ritual of ice cream and beer after climbing Cathedral Peak, and chatting with a couple whose dog had made friends with us. The woman said, "Hey, if you guys are looking for some good live music, there's a good bluegrass band playing at The Mobil tonight."

Get the hell out of here.

Live music at a gas station? This was too much. I had been to The Mobil and thought I somewhat understood its importance. But a bluegrass band? Professional musicians? What kind of musical experience could a gas station offer?

Only about 300 people showed up that night, our last night in Tuolumne. Yosemite employees, locals, and tourists like us packed the lot behind The Mobil, where the band played. You could order food if you didn't mind waiting 45 minutes to an hour. Every picnic table was filled. Dozens of parked cars filled the shoulders of Tioga Pass Road. The band, The Tresspassers, was solid.

I had not visited every convenience store in America, but as far as I was concerned, the search was over. The Mobil was everything everyone ever said it was, and more. It was a happy accident for me, a lucky side benefit of a trip to one of the greatest climbing areas in the country. The only regret I had was that the search for my holy grail was over.

--

"I can't offer you a bed," Mark said, "but you can have a couch or an empty room, roll out your sleeping bag on the floor, and sleep there. Julia's dad is dying—well, he doesn't look like he's dying when you meet him, but he's dying—so they've moved out from Connecticut to stay with us. Let me call Julia and see if it's OK, and then you can join us for dinner."

"That sounds great," I said. "I was thinking about driving north, starting to make my way into Oregon, but I'll take you up on it if it's OK with Julia." I had just dropped Tommy off at the San Francisco airport and met Mark in a bar in Hayward, across the San Mateo Bridge from SFO.

Mark is six foot four, and when he talks to you, he's more like six foot eight. It was refreshing and inspiring to sit down and talk to him. Mark was the executive director who had hired me at my old nonprofit job, and we'd stayed in touch. He is passionate and direct, and is fired up about books, stories, and anything people are doing that they're excited about.

I told him about the trip, how it started with a breakup, and how I was having a little bit of an early-thirties existential crisis, and how I'd been doing a lot of thinking about what was next for me.

"Everyone I visit, or plan to visit, is in a different place in a relationship or a family structure," I told Mark. There was me, recently single, 32. Brian was 28, single. Tommy was 31, single. Teresa, 33, single. Chris and Natalie, 29, married, and currently talking about whether or not to have kids. I was on my way to see Jack and Emelie, 32 and 34 and just moved in together after separate lives of adventure, no kids. After that, my old friend Tim, 34, in Missoula, all of a sudden a father to a 20-month old son and a 15-year-old daughter. Brian and Becca, 34, in Portland, and Brian just had a vasectomy.

Mark was a young and fiery 42. After a health scare with his wife, Julia, they decided he should leave nonprofit work and go back to the for-profit world to make more money so Julia could spend more time with their three daughters, Brooke, Sierra, and Autumn, who were eight, eight, and seven. Recently, Julia's parents, Stan and Betty, had moved in with them in their house in Castro Valley. "So there's your family, too, Mark," I said, "which is adapting to different circumstances. What's the story there?" I asked. "I'm seeing all these different models for what my life could be like next."

"Exactly," he said. "What is a life?"

Right, what is a life? Mark left our nonprofit, joined a healthcare startup, and immediately raised $6 million for them. I was living in my car.

And we were in a bar, having a great conversation, bouncing book titles back and forth, talking about different stories that pulled us in, different stories I was trying to write or wanted to write. I frantically typed his book recommendations into my phone and told him my own. "*The Only Kayak* by Kim Heacox will blow your mind. If I could write like that guy, I could die right now, Mark."

Mark lamented the fact that his new gig and the family had made it harder for him to ski and go backpacking as much as he used to, but he was still getting out some, spending a weekend in Zion a few weeks ago, taking the girls backpacking for their first time. I felt free when he said that, but then I realized he definitely wasn't unhappy, and then I felt selfish.

We drove to Mark's house, down a quiet street in Castro Valley, just in time for dinner. The driveway was a bridge across a small creek, and the yard was filled with old oak trees, a sprawling canopy over the yard. It was a nice place, simple enough to not be showy. I met Mark's whole family within five minutes: Julia, Brooke, Autumn, Sierra, Stan, Betty. The girls had a backyard and a room inside the house that was all theirs for creating, coloring, painting, playing, whatever. Mark said the neighborhood was safe enough that they spent a lot of time riding their bikes down the dead-end street, exploring like kids do, like I did during my childhood in a small town in southwest Iowa. Watching Mark and Julia and meeting the girls, it was hard to imagine those girls wouldn't have every opportunity to do whatever they wanted in life. They had parents and grandparents who cared, but they weren't coddled or spoiled; they just had enough.

We talked at the dinner table. Mark included the kids in the conversation, telling them I had just been in the Sierra Nevada, the most beautiful place in the world (and Sierra's namesake). Betty, Julia's mother, told me about a biography of Alice Walker she had just read, about how Alice Walker believed she was a writer and would not let anyone tell her otherwise. I know how she felt, Betty, I said.

A couple nights before, I was sitting at a campground with my buddy, eating macaroni and cheese, trying to get firewood to light, zipping up my sleeping bag a little more to keep the cold air out. The next night, I was in a warm home with a happy family, talking literature with a grandmother.

What is a life? Indeed, Mark.

--

"I don't know what we would do without the DVD player we have in the minivan," I've heard parents say. "We pop in *Dora the Explorer* or *Cars* or *Toy Story*," they say, "and we have peace for a couple hours. The kids are quiet."

Between the time of Kerouac and Steinbeck and now, we have changed. We have a hard time making time for real thinking, let alone real conversation. We endlessly lament this evolution, our lack of etiquette when it comes to cell phones, texting at the dinner table, using our smart phones to communicate with anyone other than the one we're sitting across from at a coffee shop. We hate that our spouse can't seem to listen to anything we say when the football game or reality TV show is on. We update our Facebook pages and Twitter feeds as things happen, relaying our experiences instantaneously to hundreds of people, but maybe cheapening the actual experience itself by doing so. We rarely sit around and just think or just talk anymore.

The driver's seat of a car might be the last sanctuary for many of us to do that, to actually think, or, if we have a passenger, to actually talk. If we aren't using our phones while driving—which most states say we shouldn't be—there is nothing left to distract us, save fiddling with the radio. Driving by yourself, if you can escape the madness of traffic and get out on a somewhat open stretch of road, invites wandering thought. It's not quite meditation, but if we minimize distraction, we can actually think. All the conveniences we have invented that trouble us during our daily lives, are off-limits and we have to return our minds to a state that has been mostly the same as long as humans have been driving.

In *Travels With Charley*, Steinbeck writes:

If one has driven a car over many years, as I have, all reactions have become automatic. One does not think about what to do. Nearly all the driving technique is deeply buried in a machine-like unconscious. This being so, a large area of the conscious mind is left free for thinking. And what do people think of when they drive? On short trips perhaps of arrival at a destination or memory of events at the place of departure. But there is left, particularly on very long trips, a large area for daydreaming or even, God help us, for thought. … Driving, I have created turtle traps in my mind, have written long, detailed letters never to be put to paper, much less sent. When the radio was on, music has stimulated memory of times and places, complete with characters and stage sets, memories so exact that every word of dialogue is recreated. And I have projected future scenes, just as complete and convincing – scenes that will never take place. I've written short stories in my mind, chuckling at my own humor, saddened or stimulated by structure or content.

Starting at the end of Mark and Julia's driveway in Castro Valley, California and going all the way to Tacoma, Washington, almost 1,000 miles and18-some hours of driving, I would have the car to myself, my music, and my thoughts.

I left early on a Sunday morning, up and driving before anyone in Mark's house was awake. I drove north in the early-morning overcast Bay scenery, through Oakland, Richmond, and Vallejo on I-5. By noon, the sun was out and I could see Mount Shasta, the tallest volcano in California, rising more than 10,000 feet above the town at its base. Two years ago, Tess and I had spent three days on a charity climb of Shasta. We trained, raised money, flew to Sacramento, and summited with a group of four other climbers. We had flown in, camped one night, met the group, spent three days on the mountain, camped another night, and flew out the next day at noon. Tess had gotten along famously with the two friends I had invited on the climb, and I remembered being so happy that I had found someone who actually liked things like mountaineering.

I drove up I-5 and watched the mountain grow bigger and bigger in my windshield. I felt like maybe I should stay there, get to know the town a little better, experience it more, something. I filled the car with gas and looked up at the mountain from town. Should I take a photo? I had been on the summit, and I still had a hard time wrapping my mind around 10,000 feet of topographic relief right there in front of my face. It was a big deal, a big event in my life with Tess.

I never knew how long to stand in front of things like Mount Shasta. The Grand Canyon, Bryce Canyon, Half Dome, El Capitan, Delicate Arch, all the incredible pieces of western landscape that we see on wall calendars— could you take them in in two minutes, or would you need ten? An hour? I had stood in front of the Mittens at Monument Valley and seen photographers set up right next to each other for an hour, while others would walk up from the parking lot, look for a minute or so, and walk into the restaurant and gift shop.

I mean, if you've seen it, have you *seen* it? In seven days, I had seen several icons of California wilderness—Mono Lake, Cathedral Peak, Half

Dome, El Capitan, the San Francisco Bay—and now I was standing here at the base of Mount Shasta, filling my car with gas and looking at the mountain from under a Shell awning.

I got in the car and headed north on I-5, saluting Shasta as I rolled onto the freeway, sweating my way into Oregon.

SIX

Chuck Klosterman's 2005 book, *Killing Ourselves to Live*, is about a 6,557-mile road trip to places where death has played an important role in music—where musicians died or committed suicide, where fatal concert disasters have happened, where Robert Johnson allegedly sold his soul to the devil. In it, Klosterman discusses the number of CDs he plans to take on his road trip:

> *It will take three hours to decide which compact discs to put in the backseat of my Tauntaun. This is the kind of quandary that keeps people like me from sleeping; I never worry about nuclear war or the economy or if we need to establish a Palestinian state, but I spend a lot of time worrying about whether I need to purchase all the less-than-stellar Rolling Stones albums from the 1980s for cataloging purposes (particularly Undercover, which includes the semi-underrated*

"Undercover of the Night"). I have 2,233 CDs. ... Right now, my eyes are

scanning their alphabetized titles, and I'm wondering how many will make the cut

for my drive across America. This decision will dictate everything. Space will be

limited, so I can only select those albums that will be undeniably essential.

I elect to bring 600.

In the days leading up to my trip, as I packed up my stuff and got

ready to abandon our Denver apartment, I had tried to put together a road

trip playlist on my iPod. What songs could I listen to for weeks without

getting tired of them?

A properly crafted road trip playlist is varied but heavily populated

with songs that capture the rhythm of the road. Push "play" on a song and

imagine looking out your windshield, dotted lines clicking past your wheels.

Does it feel right, encourage thought, introspection, nostalgia? What will

make me *think* out there?

Contemplative lyrics. Acoustic guitars. slide guitars. Storytelling.

Lyrics about life, traveling, knowing, not knowing, going, *leaving.*

I am assured yes/I am assured yes/I am assured that peace will come to me ...

I see it swell/like a story in me to tell ...

I'm changin all my strings/gonna write another traveling song ...

I'm just walking the miles, every once in a while I'll get a ride/I'm thumbing my

way back to heaven …

Somewhere on a desert highway/She rides a Harley-Davidson …

I'm going up the country/baby don't you wanna go …

Honey we could be in Kansas/By the time the snow begins to thaw …

We drove out to the desert just to lie down beneath this bowl of stars/We stand

up in the palace like it's the last of the great pioneer town bars …

Like a band of gypsies we go down the highway …

We run like a river/runs to the sea …

I wish that I knew what I know now/When I was younger …

I had time to pick 740 songs.

The music is so, so important on a long trip, almost as important as gas in the tank. You can choose to pass the hours listening to books on tape, podcasts, talk radio—but none of that provides a soundtrack to what you're experiencing. Do you want to watch your own adventure unfold while listening to someone talk, or listening to someone sing? You can't predict the moments when it will happen, but sometimes, say, when the opening funky guitar chords of Isaac Hayes's "Hung Up On My Baby" surprise you through your stereo speakers, you turn the volume knob up a little bit and smile, nod and say to yourself, Yes, this is what I needed. Right now. Heading north on I-5 between Portland and Tacoma, I look east, hoping for a glimpse of Mount

Rainier.

Part of Kerouac's story in *On the Road* is about jazz, the music in the hearts of the Beats, the music decent folk weren't comfortable listening to back then. The book is rife with descriptions of the music, and as a writer, I wished I could write about the music I loved with the energy Kerouac drives into his writing about jazz. Even Kerouac's writing, the stream-of-consciousness and improvisation of the entire book, is inspired by jazz.

Chances are, a song from a road trip will brand itself onto a memory, a memory of a trip you took with a friend, of a time in your life or a feeling you had then—sad or happy or free or innocent or whatever. And every time you hear that song, it can take you back to that trip, your arm out the window, wind blowing through the car; maybe you were talking about women, men, life, death, the future, something else; maybe you were talking about nothing, just having your own peace in the front seat, your friend having his or hers in the passenger seat, for a few minutes. Listening to that song.

The Five Greatest Road Trip Songs of All Time are:

5. "Graceland," Willie Nelson

4. "Isis," Bob Dylan

3. "Dark Matter," Andrew Bird

2. "Golden," My Morning Jacket

1. "The Valley Town," Elliott Brood

Jack and I sat down at a table at Katie Downs Waterfront Restaurant, a few feet from the water of Puget Sound in Tacoma, and I looked up to see Mount Rainier for the first time. All the way back in Denver in July, I had packed mountaineering boots and crampons in my car, knowing somewhere in the back of my mind that if I got the opportunity, I wanted to get up there and try to climb it.

Rainier doesn't fit the mold of what constitutes a mountain, not to the mind of someone who's lived in Denver for six years. Colorado's Front Range is gradual, rising from the plains—you can drive up and into and over the mountains, over the Continental Divide, in about three hours. Rainier, the giant, hulking, snowy mass, a single mountain rising behind the cities of Tacoma and Seattle, is like another goddamn *planet*, sitting right there. A beautiful, dangerous, and fierce white ghost creeping up on the horizon.

Jack was uneasy about his recent move to Tacoma from Denver.

"Everybody just keeps saying, 'It's getting better' when they talk about Tacoma," Jack said.

"What does that mean?" I asked. "What did it used to be like? Kosovo?"

Two years before, when I'd met Jack, he'd been flying all over the world, spending all the money he'd made in Antarctica. Everything he owned was sitting in his tiny Volkswagen hatchback at a friend's house in Denver. At the end of that summer, we were scheduled to take four black and Latino teenagers from Portland on their first backpacking trip ever, in the Wallowa Mountains in eastern Oregon. Jack flew in from Hawaii the night before, less than eight hours before we met the kids.

Jack graduated from nursing school in Denver in May, moved his stuff to Tacoma the week after, and then spent the next two and a half months climbing in Switzerland and bike touring Spain and Portugal with Emelie. Emelie was a professor at the University of Puget Sound, and Jack, a new nurse, could work from any hospital in America; so he moved to Washington instead of asking her to move to Colorado. They got back from Portugal three days before I got there. He was nervous about trying to meet new friends, nervous about the grey skies when they would move in permanently in October, nervous he'd never really like the town.

"I don't have any network here, which is kind of tough," he said. Jack has light blonde hair and is sturdily built, a former paramedic, wilderness therapy instructor, and one winter, a firefighter in Antarctica. He'd been all over the world and lived an adventurous life on a shoestring budget. He'd climbed in Switzerland, Alaska, all over the western U.S.; bicycled from Alaska to Colorado; backpacked across Iceland; bike toured in Russia, the Dominican Republic, and Mongolia; and had done about a million things he probably hadn't told me about yet, because they hadn't come up in conversation. He didn't brag and didn't try to impress you with his travel resume. He'd rather talk about the rock climbing he did last weekend.

One of my favorite Jack stories was about a grizzly bear in the Yukon Territory, where he moved the year after he graduated high school to help a man run sled dogs. The first time I heard it, we were sitting around a campfire in the Wallowas with the kids from Portland.

During his job in the Yukon, Jack stayed in a small town and had to walk to work every day and home every night. After he had done the walk a few times, a few folks in town figured out that an old grizzly bear had been getting lazy and coming into town for food at night, along the same road Jack walked to get to and from his job. It was time to end the bear's dumpster-diving before someone got hurt; so one night a couple men waited for the bear with hunting rifles, and when it appeared, they shot it to death.

Jack had helped skin the bear, and when they pulled back the skin on its skull, they found seven bullets embedded in the bone.

"Only two of those bullets were from the two guys' guns that night, and none of the seven bullets in the skull actually killed the bear," Jack said to the group of teenagers, all of whom had a new definition for the word "tough."

I felt bad for Jack, all alone in Tacoma, no job yet, and no one to go climbing with. But he and Emelie had dated long-distance for two years, and it was time, he said. She was as adventurous as he was, but had a more structured work schedule. Emelie was in a bluegrass band, had played in a successful ska band in college, and was game for anything. She'd joined Jack on a climb of Mount Hood, the bike tour in the Dominican Republic, and the most recent bike trip in Spain and Portugal. And now he was moving into a nice little house in Tacoma with her and making a go of it.

Kids were basically off the table at this point, Jack said, as we ate. Emelie was 34, and they had just moved in together, so they had to concentrate on seeing if the relationship would work first before thinking about kids. I heard him. That idea wasn't so bad, I thought. A childless relationship with a person who was interesting and adventurous, maybe intriguing enough to spend the rest of your life getting to know her without the distractions of raising a family. Would that be lonely, though, I thought and didn't say. What is a life?

--

Jack and I topped out on Ingalls Peak at 5 p.m., very late to be on the summit of any peak. But the forecast was 0 percent chance of rain, and there we were looking west from the craggy top, and Rainier's I'm-so-huge-I-create-my-own-weather bulk didn't even have a cloud on it. To the north, the Cascades spread out all the way to Canada, and to the east, Mount Stuart dominated everything, the largest chunk of exposed rock in the Lower 48, a sinister and beautiful wedge of black.

Whenever I touched the summit of any mountain, I always said or thought the words "halfway to the car." Most mountaineering accidents happen on the descent, not on the climb. I don't know, you let your guard down, get lazy, get tired. You make mistakes.

We rappelled three times, then ran out of places to anchor our rope. We were at the top of a cliff and the only way down was a snowfield to the west. It was steep, terrain where you'd want a pair of crampons or an ice axe to descend. If you have at least an ice axe when you're walking down steep snow, and you slip, you flip around and dig the pick into the snow and kick your toes until you slow down and stop. The ice axe is really your only seat belt on a snowfield or a glacier.

For the snowfield on Ingalls, I had no seat belt. I was wearing a pair of running shoes, not even stiff enough to kick steps in the snow to climb down. Goddammit. I picked up a couple rocks, shaped like slivers of a pie and hopefully long enough to dig into the snow and stop me if my feet slipped. I eyeballed the snowfield; it must have been 35-40 degrees, ending in a heinous-looking pile of broken rocks, the kind of thing you wouldn't jump onto from four feet above, let alone want to slide into from 40 feet up. Impacting loose talus at any speed is medically not a good idea and not fun, and if you spare your ankles and lower legs, I wouldn't count on keeping your balance and not flipping onto your back or side and getting hurt even worse.

How did I feel about this, I wondered. I climb, right? Like I say, some people drink to forget about things for a while, some people go shopping for new shoes. I climb. Keep telling yourself that, meathead, and you will keep getting into situations like this. Next thing I do on this trip in the outdoors, I'm bringing a goddamn ice axe. I don't care if it's a walk on the beach. This is the second snowfield I've had to cross or descend with nothing but a pair of sharp rocks in my hands. Fuck me.

I started to kick steps, my running shoes flexing on impact. It was a joke. I hammered my toes into the slope, hoping to make small shelves to stand on, and hoping those held. Some did. I'd made it maybe 10 feet down, 40 feet of slippery snow beneath me ending in a pile of rocky pain, when my left foot blew out. The step I'd kicked had suddenly disintegrated under it. Everything in my body tightened, and I dug the rocks in, and five years disappeared off my life as my heart leapt into my throat. I hung on.

Ten minutes later, my shoes were soaked, and I finally reached my left foot down onto the talus, chucking my trusty rocks into a pile. Jack made faster time, climbing down in the steps I had kicked in the snow. That's all I needed for a week, maybe more, I thought. My nerves were shot.

We started to walk down the talus, stepping, hopping, and butt-sliding from boulder to boulder. The scary stuff was behind us. I started imagining a bottle of Gatorade in two hours. Lemon-lime, no, orange, no, lemon-lime.

Then, FUCK.

I got lazy, complacent, and I stepped onto an uneven rock with my left foot. It flipped, and then I flipped.

Jack said later it looked like I fell *up*, then down. I don't even know what that means.

All points of contact were off the ground for a half-second, no feet or hands touching earth, and then. Wham. I slammed into a rock, left ribcage taking most of the impact and blowing a throaty scream out of my diaphragm. My kneecaps and left upper arm landed next, and it was like someone hit them with a hammer. Maybe my head hit, too, I don't know, but I still had my helmet on. I heard Jack yell, "Holy shit!" from behind me.

I scrambled back onto my feet immediately, as if that would make it better. I waited for whatever happens when you start bleeding internally—I don't know, I imagine a warm feeling starts to spread throughout your abdomen. Something had to have exploded inside when I landed on that rock. I took a breath, then another one, as my knees and arm flooded with pain. Deep breath this time. Long as nothing was wrong in my torso, I could walk, even though it felt like someone just hit both my knees with a baseball bat.

"I can breathe OK, so that must be a good sign," I said, panting. I moved downhill, hyper-aware and overly careful now, adrenaline flushing everything. Jack began to get ahead of me. Once off the talus, we stepped onto the trail, still an hour or more back to the car and less than an hour of daylight left. We crossed Headlight Creek and I stepped off the trail to pee, walking in the opposite direction of a group of mountain goats that grazed upstream.

Mountain goats love pee. Our urine is salty, and animals love salt. At high altitudes, we pee on rocks instead of plants, because mountain goats will eat pee-salted plants until an alpine meadow is barren. So I walked away from the goats because I wanted a little privacy.

It was as if the sound of my zipper was a dinner bell. A narrow white face, curious, popped over a ridge 20 feet from my crotch. Then another one. Jesus Christ, talk about stage fright or performance anxiety. They approached confidently.

A few months earlier, the National Park Service had advised hikers not to urinate near trails in Olympic National Park, after a mountain goat attacked and killed a 63-year-old man on a trail there. It was the only known fatal mountain goat attack in the park's history.

As the two goats walked toward me, I pictured the headline, then a photo of me splayed out, pants at my ankles, penis exposed, having been gored to death with my pants down in the shadow of Mount Stuart as the sun set on the Enchantments. I zipped my pants and briskly walked away. I could wait.

We trotted down the trail as the sky went dark, clicked on our headlamps, and walked down the last three miles in complete darkness, talking about the feast of gas station snacks we'd have when we got back to civilization.

There was this girl.

I had spent the afternoon shooting clay pigeons with a 20-gauge shotgun with Jack and Emelie, the second time I'd ever shot a gun in my life. I had not showered since Wednesday and it was Saturday. My hair had blown into a sloppy mess of frizz and Shirley Temple curls.

The restaurant walls were covered in posters from my childhood, now hipster irony: Isaiah Thomas, Michael Jordan, Iron Maiden, Eric B. and Rakim, Hulk Hogan. We looked over the menu to decide what kind of pizza to order. And there was this girl. At a booth across the room. Black hair, strapless top, long tan legs, shorts, part of a tattoo snaking up out of her top onto a tan shoulder. Did I say tan, legs, shoulders, tattoo? She was incredible. She was 22 years old? Maybe 24. And she was looking. At. Me.

I made eye contact with her once and smiled slightly. This was the extent of my flirting technique. I last went on a date in 2003 and I couldn't even remember how I asked the girl out. That was eight years ago.

What was I going to do in Olympia, Washington, a city I didn't want to live in? Go and talk to this girl who is in her early twenties, in a completely different place in life than me? I wasn't going to move there and start dating someone who was in college. Maybe if she was in grad school.

Then she was looking at me again. Should I go talk to her? What would I say? "Do you come here often?" I made eye contact with her again.

What am I doing. If she was indeed checking me out, this was the most attractive woman who had ever checked me out. All downhill from here.

We sat down at a booth and waited for our pizza. I wasn't going to go talk to a 20-year-old college student in a pizza place in Olympia, Washington, even if she was the most attractive woman who had ever showed the slightest interest in me, without actually talking to me. Her back was to me, a couple of booths away. Then she turned around to look at me. She turned *around* to look at me. This was important. What was I doing? Could she be the one? What if this was the most beautiful woman I would ever have a chance with, and I just sat over here doing nothing?

I was less than two months out of my last relationship, and had been in relationships for the past 12 years, on and off. Never really single. I needed more time. Didn't I? I mean, when I was ready, five or six months after Tess and I split, would incredible-looking women still notice me at pizza restaurants in college towns? And then, would I have the balls to go up and talk to them? Would it ever happen again?

What if she wasn't interesting, though. What if I wasn't interesting? What if she really was 22? What if she was 22, and all she cared about was watching punk bands at bars in Olympia? What the hell was I going to do, ask her if she had plans tomorrow night, so I could go take a shower and try to smell better and take her out on a date? Then what?

What if I was just too scared to go up and talk to a woman I didn't know in a place I didn't know, even if it could be the best thing that ever happened to me? And what if I never could.

Then she left, and it was over. I had to learn how to do this.

--

I looked over the steering wheel across Washington's farmland on the east side of the Cascades on I-90. I was sweating, again. Leaning forward for a while seemed to help circulate some air, cooling the hot spot between my back and the seat. Then when I leaned back, the sweat on my shirt had cooled a few degrees, and it seemed to cool my back a little. That was my system. Gold and green fields passed by at 80 mph, and it felt like 20 mph.

Kids. Do I want kids? The next woman I date is going to want to know this, I am sure of it.

I'm 32. If I did want kids, wouldn't I be sure by now? Wouldn't someone else's child smile at me, like my nephew Max, and something inside would click, and I would just know?

It's a big deal now. With my wife, it wasn't on the table until she used it to leverage our divorce, assuming I'd never budge on having kids with her. I probably would have. With Tess, it was going to happen eventually. I was warming up to it. I started to have a relationship with her nephew, playing with him when we visited her sister. I could see myself doing everything in fatherhood, aside from changing diapers. And that, I would just have to do when the time came. Tess was five years younger than me, essentially giving me time until I was in my mid-thirties before we had to "settle down" and have a baby or two. What now?

If I meet a girl who's 32 or 33, or even 31, and we decide to have kids, it's got to happen in the next four, three, or two years. Now the clock is ticking.

So do I decide first that yes, I want kids, or no, I don't want kids, and then start dating? Or is that something I can decide on my own? Who says I'm not going to fall for a woman and be so head over heels in love with her that I can't imagine NOT having kids with her? I don't know how this works. Apparently I've never been with the right woman.

What do I say in a personals ad? "Not 100 percent sure I want kids, but I'm sure after I meet you, I will want to have babies with you, unless you're not into having kids, in which case I am not, either. But if we change our minds when we're 40, we can always adopt." Jesus Christ.

I know I want to drink more coffee, and I know I want to climb mountains and listen to old-school hip hop and eat chocolate. Shouldn't it be that easy to decide?

SEVEN

The green mountains to the south of Missoula took shape in my passenger window as I rolled up the Bitterroot Valley on Highway 93. I waited for the ones I would recognize from all my time looking up at them from town—Mount Dean Stone, Mount Sentinel, Mount Jumbo. My first mountains as an adult, the first time I could see something like that and appreciate the majesty of it all, respect it. Montana was where I had dipped my toe into the mountain world for the first time, backpacking in Glacier National Park, hiking to the top of peaks near Missoula in the fall, catching the bug for peak bagging, flipping through guidebooks, checking maps for the next high place I wanted to go.

I drove closer to the center of the city, waiting for the skyline to click into a familiar place that matched my memory of it. How long ago was it that I left here? Seven years before, the last week of May, I'd driven out of town on I-90 West, headed toward Seattle and eventually Phoenix, to my then-girlfriend, who was now three years my ex-wife. I hadn't been back to Missoula since then.

I knew where it was in my mind for the past seven years, but I wasn't sure I wanted to be there again. I felt something like nostalgia, but more sad.

When I arrived in August 2002, I was 23 years old, fresh out of substance abuse treatment for alcohol, a pack-a-day smoker, depressed, desperate for a new life, and worried I wasn't good enough for the graduate program at the School of Journalism at the University of Montana. Missoula, sitting at the foot of Mount Sentinel, whose grassy west face sweeps down to the UM campus behind the football stadium, was like no place I'd ever been before. Deer would walk down from the mountain at night and munch on grass on the quad in front of the university president's office. Just across I-90 from Mount Sentinel is Mount Jumbo, another enormous grassy mountain, and the Clark Fork River cuts in between the two along the interstate, down Hellgate Canyon.

Anywhere in town, the view of those two mountains was a shock to a kid from Iowa whose horizons had been dominated by nothing bigger than grain elevators since he was born. Everyone walked with dogs off leashes, everywhere; and when dogs weren't allowed into a shop or a bar, they waited contently outside, sitting on the sidewalk. On Higgins Avenue, there were three coffee shops, none of which was a Starbucks. Drive-thru espresso booths seemed to be on every other block. How could coffee be this important? Why didn't I have a beard?

There were two mountaineering shops, Pipestone Mountaineering and The Trail Head, within four blocks of each other. And people rode their bikes on the street, with the cars, unlike in Iowa, where the only reason you rode a bike anywhere was if you had been slapped with a DUI and lost your driver's license. Then you pedaled down the sidewalk.

The U.S. Forest Service office for the Northern region was a block off Broadway, and every third car that cruised past had a rack for snowboards, skis, mountain bikes, or kayaks, or all of the above. The largest U.S. base for training smokejumpers, people who parachuted in to fight forest fires, was in Missoula.

Most people dressed in ski jackets or fleeces and Carhartts. There were beards, long hair, dreadlocks, and cowboy hats on actual cowboys, and there were license plates from everywhere, except Iowa.

In 2002, I didn't climb, I didn't ski, and I didn't even own a decent pair of hiking boots. That didn't last long.

--

Tim and I pedaled bikes down the bike path next to the Clark Fork River on our way to the campus.

"How does it feel to be back?" he asked.

You know, I said, I really wanted to feel something, and I was nervous I wouldn't feel anything. Maybe it's because I don't know anyone here anymore, besides you and maybe two other people, so it's really just a city I lived in for a couple years.

But it was so formative when I was there. The first year of grad school was probably the hardest of my life. I was sad, depressed, had no real direction or sense of identity, and by the time I left, I had started to develop a new identity. I had discovered the mountains in a very small way, and would grow my identity in them over the next few years, hiking, backpacking, learning to climb ice and rock, and skiing in the backcountry.

When I left Missoula, I had published a single story in a magazine, *IDAHO Magazine,* which paid $40. Except I told them I'd rather have 12 copies of the magazine mailed to me instead. I was so proud of that story. So I never got a check for my first article. Over the next few years, I got a handful of stories published in small publications. And now, seven years later, I told Tim, if you walked into a bookstore, you could pick up copies of *Climbing* magazine and *Backpacker,* and my stories would be in both of them. No, really, this month's issue. I was proud.

I had moved to town not knowing how to do anything in the outdoors and not knowing how to write, and now I was writing for national outdoor magazines. All those people I was so enamored of when I moved here, with the ski jackets and roof racks on their cars, living to kayak or climb or ski? I was now one of them. I had been in a dozen towns like Missoula, where everyone had a roof rack and everyone climbed or hiked or skied or mountain biked, and I knew my way around them; and I knew my way around the mountains. I still couldn't grow a beard, though.

"Yeah, so it's kind of strange being back," I said.

Tim and I parked the bikes at a bike rack at the trailhead for the M, a 50-foot tall concrete white letter 620 feet up Mount Sentinel. The main trail switchbacks 13 times on its way up, with several benches at the turns for those needing a rest on the way up. My first time here nine years before, I had battled up the trail to get to the top. My legs and lungs, more accustomed to sitting on barstools in Iowa and smoking, could barely handle all the uphill walking. It was the first trail I had ever tried to hike as an adult. I must have walked up to the M a couple dozen times while getting my master's degree, more and more after I had started hiking into the mountains around Missoula on the weekends. It was a good, short hike for maintaining fitness for bigger things, to remind the legs what it was like to walk on steep, uneven terrain.

Tim could have gone without hiking up to the M, I could tell—it was a cliché thing for visitors to do their first time in Missoula, and the trail was always packed with people. But I wanted to go back, since it represented the start of my life in the mountains. I hadn't been on the trail in so long, and it was a special place. Tim took us up the back trail to the top, the steeper route that had no one on it. It was easy.

We topped out on the upper edge of the concrete M in a few short minutes, and I got my camera out and started trying to catch the sunset as it dropped over the rolling mountains west of town. Tim and I talked about relationships, about what had happened with Tess and me, about how his life was now. He grabbed my camera, made a few adjustments, and nailed a sunset photo far better than I could have. He was happy, he said, though being a dad was sometimes a challenge, as was being the only person in the relationship bringing in any money.

The last time I saw him was at my wedding in 2007, four years before. He was single then, and maybe kind of lost like I was now; and he'd run his rental car out of gas on the way to the Vegas airport, missing his flight.

Tim and Heidi met while helping a mutual friend move into a new apartment in Missoula, and he didn't make a move at first. They met again a few weeks later at an art gallery opening, hung out with a group of friends afterward, and Tim thought, "I've got to get an angle" with this tall, dark-haired woman. Someone mentioned that Tim knew how to play the guitar, and Heidi said, "Maybe you could give me lessons? My dad gave me a guitar for Christmas." There was his angle. He said yes, although he hadn't played in a few years.

When she offered him a ride home from a gathering a day later, he gave her directions to his apartment building. They pulled up in front and Heidi said, "Which one is yours?" He pointed to his apartment, and she said,

"Oh, you mean my apartment?" She had lived there a few years before. He invited her up to see the place. She poked around, chuckling to herself, and got ready to leave, saying "Hey, a bunch of us are getting together at a friend's tonight. You should come over. Bring your guitar."

So he did, and he played for the group of friends. First time he'd played in a couple years, and she liked it. She gave him a ride home later and asked for his number so they could get together again. She got out of the car and gave him a hug, a real one. First hugs are awesome, Tim said, like the world is in your arms.

Now he was 34, father of a 20-month old boy, Jasper, and dad/stepdad to a 15-year-old girl named Ursula. When he talked about the ways parenthood had changed him, I could not believe he was the same guy I used to smoke cigarettes with outside The Raven in Missoula, back when he had a little more hair and I had fewer lines on my face.

"It's forced me to be a dick sometimes, and to take a stand, and say no, you can't do that," he said. Ursula's father was killed when Tim's girlfriend, Heidi, was six months pregnant. When Tim came into the picture, he learned to fill the father role. That spring, when Ursula felt overwhelmed by schoolwork and finals at the same time as her swimming season was wrapping up, she wanted to just not show up for her final meets and concentrate on school.

"This is the part of someone's life where they begin behavior patterns that last for the rest of their lives," Tim said. "You can't just quit something when it gets tough, right?" And that's what they told Ursula — Mom and Tim/Dad. Tim had attended one semester of our graduate program at the School of Journalism at the University of Montana before he figured out it wasn't for him. Later he finished a year of law school before dropping out. But that wasn't because things had gotten tough. He was tough. His first-ever backpacking trip was a 6-month thru-hike of the Appalachian Trail.

Tim and Heidi lived in a rented two-bedroom house in Missoula and Tim developed software from his home office. Before he met Heidi, he did short-term contract software development and spent summers in fire lookouts in Idaho, staying for weeks in a tiny tower and looking over miles and miles of mountains all day, with no one to talk to.

"You know what I remember about Missoula?" I said to Tim as the sunset exploded over the city lights. "I remember the time you and I hiked up and over the top of Mount Sentinel, and it must have gotten dark way before we got to the top, and we ran down the front toward campus in the dark, and I remember sitting here and watching the lights of a plane flying down the Bitterroot all the way across the valley to the airport. That was great."

Tim and I used to take off whenever we had a few hours and just drive out of Missoula in any direction. Even when the weather wasn't great for hiking, trailheads were snowed in, we could head out of town and take in some Montana through the car windows, open just a crack so we could ash our cigarettes. Down 93 in front of the Bitterroot Mountains, west on 12 along Lolo Creek, up Highway 200 to the National Bison Range, north on 83 to Seeley Lake.

We talked about Montana once on the phone after I had been gone for a couple years, and Tim explained that he thought the mountains were different there—you weren't in them when you drove, like in the Colorado Rockies. You drove along the valleys in the middle and the mountains scooped up on either side, with all that space in the middle, drawing your eyes way out there. Big Sky, I suppose. I just remembered the place with golden light on all of it, like you remember a childhood home or the first months of falling in love with someone.

Coming back, it was great, but I had seen so much since I had been gone. Nothing had changed, but my eyes had.

--

The fall of my final year in school at UM, Tim and I took off nearly every Saturday morning to hike up nearby peaks. The last one we tried before the snow started falling in earnest up high was a mountain called Grave Peak, and we had turned around in view of the summit, maybe because it was starting to rain, or get late, or because I was coming down with a cold.

After that, I had read Norman Maclean's story, *USFS 1919: The Ranger, the Cook, and a Hole in the Sky*, and realized that as a Forest Service employee, Maclean had sat atop Grave Peak as a fire lookout, a few years before the building was built. Since then, I had always wanted to go back, if for nothing more than to make a pilgrimage to a place one of my heroes had once been. In that story, Maclean writes:

By the middle of that summer when I was seventeen I had yet to see myself become part of a story. I had as yet no notion that life every now and then becomes literature — not for long, of course, but long enough to be what we best remember, and often enough so that what we eventually come to mean by life are those moments when life, instead of going sideways, backwards, forward, or nowhere at all, lines out straight, tense and inevitable, with a complication, climax, and, given some luck, a purgation, as if life had been made and not happened.

My sense was not that every now and then—as Norman Maclean writes—but *always*, life is literature. As long as you see your life as a story, it's just a matter of picking out the right pieces to tell. The storyteller always lines it out straight, tense, and inevitable, and tells the story, which had indeed been made and not happened. That was what I wanted to do.

A couple weeks before my visit, I had asked Tim if he would like to get out of town for a day, go hike somewhere, do something. Kind of like the good old days or whatever. I suggested Grave Peak. We could go finish the hike we started almost exactly eight years ago, when we were different people, both of us lost young men living in Missoula. Now he was a dad and I was a lost, only-kind-of-young man. Sure thing, he said.

Why were we trying to hike up there in the first place, back in 2003, Tim asked. I didn't remember. He began to rifle through his bookshelves for a guidebook, and I noticed all the books I had given him on my way out of town seven years before. It must have been in the Bitterroot hiking guidebook, Tim said, which was lost somewhere after some friend had borrowed it. We found a map online.

"We can take my car to the trailhead," Tim said. "We just won't have any music—I can't get my iPod to work in there."

"Nah, I'll drive," I said. "You drove last time."

An hour up a snaking dirt road, we parked in a dirt pullout on a ridge above the Walton lakes and started to walk a ridge at 11 a.m. Hard to get an early start when you have an infant at home. We were above the trees in minutes, and the sun was already high and hot. We connected three ridges, the last a scramble over loose rock choked with trees, and I waited for Tim to walk the final few feet to the lookout.

We moved a bolt out of the latch and walked into the lookout, which was boarded up and long out of use. It was different being in a place like that with Tim. I tried to get him to tell me about the life up there. He liked to sit and do a mental map of all the surrounding mountains—let's see, that must be Oregon Butte over there, which would make that ridge such-and-such mountain and those over there would be the such-and-such mountains. I imagined him doing this for hours every day, just staring out the windows in a lookout, watching for a column of smoke somewhere, the one moment defining the long months of that job. Jesus Christ, what did you do up here?

"All the alone time forced me to deal with a lot of stuff I didn't really want to deal with," he said. "Stuff from my past, my family, you know." I imagined. There was no more complete lack of distraction than there was in the job of a lookout. He was a modern-day monk, without the task of praying 12 hours a day. Just look for fires, and look inside your head, and try not to go crazy up on a mountain.

"I have to get back in a lookout," he kept saying. How could that happen, I wondered, for the provider of a family, with health insurance and a 20-month-old son? You can walk away from a job when it's just you. You can't walk away from a family, a 20-month-old, just because you want to go meditate in a little house in the sky. Maybe he was just saying it as a hypothetical, the way people dream about that ski vacation they never take. Or maybe he would line things up so he could do it again. Who knew?

His second summer as a lookout, he and Heidi had just started dating, and he would come down from the lookout for his two days off every seven days to see her. He would literally run the eight miles down 5,000 vertical feet. Since he would announce via the Forest Service radio when he'd start the hike down and when he'd get to the trailhead, people started noticing, and he became something of a legend for his descent times—his fastest time all season was 90 minutes. Eight miles in 90 minutes, down a vertical mile. And then he'd drive four and a half hours to Polson, Montana to see his new girl.

Remember that, I imagined Heidi saying to Tim, remember when you used to run down off that mountain to see me? I liked that story.

--

I toured the new University of Montana journalism building, making arrangements to come in as a guest speaker for the magazine writing class. The old journalism building was now dedicated to geography, and the campus newspaper office where I'd spent so much time was no more. The computer lab where I'd sat for hours and hours writing my thesis project, and then an hour defending it to my thesis committee, was now a classroom. I wish there were a word for the feeling nostalgia puts in your chest, when it's that big. I was in and out of the building in less than 30 seconds, brushing my hand on the railing along the steps on the south side of the building where I'd smoked a million cigarettes between writing and editing news stories.

The place where I'd learned to write was gone, as was the desperate guy who didn't know what to do with himself when he moved to Missoula. There was probably a photo of both of them somewhere, that I could look at and try to remember all the details.

Later that afternoon, I hiked up to the M again on the same trail as Tim and I had taken on my first night back in Missoula. The back way. I quickly caught a couple heading up the trail for their first time ever, the girl out of breath and protesting, the guy telling her that the end was "just up there." They stepped off the trail to let me pass, and I asked them how they were doing. Out of shape, she said. I said something like Yeah, it's pretty steep, isn't it, and smiled.

Maybe it was her first time on Mount Sentinel, or her first time in Missoula; or, maybe like me not so long ago, it was her first time doing any walking on a trail. I remember taking water bottles up there, battling bursting quads, and wondering if I'd ever catch my breath, if it would ever get any easier.

It was easier, finally. I looked down at my jeans and sandals. Hundreds of miles in dozens of places had passed under my feet since I lived here—the Grand Canyon, the Sierras, the Tetons, the Wallowas, Canyonlands, the Rocky Mountains in Colorado, hours and hours of walking with a backpack on my back. This was like going back and taking my first childhood bicycle out for a spin. It felt small, but it was still great.

Rockin' Rudy's, a record store in Missoula, used to sell these T-shirts that said "Missoula, Montana: A Place, Sort Of." I never knew what they were supposed to mean, but I picked one up at a thrift store just before I graduated and held onto it as a souvenir of my time there. Eventually, I got rid of the shirt. I didn't wear it because it didn't fit quite right.

Down the M Trail, I understood. Missoula, as revered and romantic as it was in my memory, wasn't a place I could go back to. It was a time in my life and the catalyst for an incredible transformation, but I couldn't go visit that. Maybe I was sad that I couldn't walk into those old buildings and see that sad, scared kid who was wondering what it would take to be a writer someday. That could have been the feeling in my chest when I walked down the stairs of the old journalism building.

--

I woke up on a picnic table at the northernmost Forest Service campground on Rock Creek Road, south of I-90 and a few miles east of Missoula, the smell of pine trees in my nose. A guy at the campground had told me they'd had some moose walk through the campground a few nights before, and I thought, you know, I'll just spread my sleeping bag out on this picnic table and cut down the risk of getting stepped on by a moose in the middle of the night.

I unzipped my sleeping bag and sat up, rubbed my eyes, pulled knots out of my hair. I popped out of my bag, slid my sandals on, and walked over to the car to put in my contact lenses, and brush my teeth. I lit my backpacking stove on the table to heat a pot of water for coffee and oatmeal, and the low exhale of the flame was the only sound in the campground. I put the hood up on my down jacket. It was already cool in Montana, the Thursday before Labor Day.

I sat on the top of the table and ate oatmeal, my dirty feet on the bench. I was down in the middle of a gentle, winding pine-studded canyon that Rock Creek Road followed for 50 miles along the creekbed. Rock Creek was famous for fly fishing, and I could imagine standing in the water and watching it roll by on an early summer morning, before the sun peeked over the mountains to the east.

I had been traveling, homeless, for 32 days. A month. Sleeping on a picnic table was all right, and keeping my toothbrush on the dashboard of my car, that was all right too.

Two months since I had seen Tess, left our home behind. I was alone, maybe a little lonely. But we weren't as fresh in my mind anymore; thinking of her didn't cut fresh, hot pain in my stomach. It was a dull sadness. Did I miss her? I did, still. But it felt like the sun was starting to come up a little bit.

East on I-90 then south on I-15 toward Idaho, dry, golden mountains were my walls, cresting above the valleys between. All these Montana mountains, the ones nobody cares about because they aren't famous, aren't Mount Rainier or Mount Hood or even Longs Peak. No one has ever heard of them. What's the tremendous peak across I-15 from Dell, Montana? Must be 3,000 feet above the road, and no one's ever stopped to take a photo of it. There are hundreds just like it all over the West, the peaks no one notices, making up the driving scenery where you can do all your thinking.

EIGHT

Over and over for weeks, I had played Dire Straits' *Romeo and Juliet*. I would take my iPod into my sleeping bag, plug my headphones into my ears, and listen to Mark Knopfler gently rip my heart out of my chest. And I fell asleep, thinking maybe tomorrow I'd feel one or two percent better.

The song isn't about Shakespeare's Romeo and Juliet, but about two people who fall in love, and in Knopfler's words, "it was just that the time was wrong." And it was about me. And Tess. And maybe me and my ex-wife, too.

It was something about the guitar, the arc of the love story, and Knopfler's humble singing, especially when he takes the voice of Romeo who says,

I can't do the talks

Like they talk on the TV

I can't do a love song

Like the way it's meant to be

I can't do everything

But I'll do anything for you

Romeo, in the song, is just a normal guy like me, like you, like all of us, who aims for the stars and wants to make a woman happy, a woman he knows is too good for him—the woman all of us dream about. The next line, every time Knopfler sings it, is perfect in nailing all of us hopeless romantic men so dead-on it feels like somebody just punched you in the stomach:

I can't do anything except be in love with you

And then it's over for Romeo and Juliet, like my relationship, another time I was in love and failed. Mark Knopfler pushes the words out with the pain of a thousand heartbroken men:

And all I do is miss you

And the way we used to be

This, I thought, is the most heartbreaking song of all time. I didn't question why I was doing it, listening to this song over and over. I had a couple dozen other sad songs at my disposal, all these hurt singers' voices with me in the car or in my headphones at night: *I want you back. I thought I saw your face today. If you died would I care whether or not you're gone/ Would I hear it in passing conversation. You were the only answer. If I weren't leaving/ would I catch you dreaming.* All of them.

Then a friend sent me an episode of *This American Life* called *Break-Up*. In the episode, writer Starlee Kine tells the story of her breakup and how she dealt with it by listening to breakup songs—in particular, Phil Collins' song *Against All Odds.*

She says:

If I thought I was in a Phil Collins phase before, it was nothing compared to what came next. I was no longer listening to his songs for pleasure, but for pain. They were breakup songs. Hearing them was the only thing that made me feel better. And by better, I mean worse.

There's something so satisfying about listening to sad songs. They're like how you would actually be spending your day if you were allowed to break down and sob and grab hold of everyone you met. They make you feel less alone with your crazy thoughts. They don't judge you; in fact, they understand you. A breakup song won't ever suggest you try online dating, or that you're better off without him. They tell you that you're worse without him, which is exactly what you want to hear, because it's how you feel.

I didn't want to be cheered up, I didn't want to bounce back, I didn't want to meet someone new. I wanted to wallow — big time, deeply, and with the least amount of perspective possible. And the only way to do that was by turning off my phone and turning up the sad, sad music.

That's what I had been doing for a month.

But then one day, I had stopped listening to breakup songs. I hadn't consciously stopped; I just noticed that I had. I felt better about the end, about Tess moving on without me. The future still worried me, consumed much of my thinking, but I was putting my two and a half years with Tess in a good place, settling up and being OK with losing, and losing kind of big.

--

Highway 191, south of Jackson, Wyoming, I started to think about the possibility of dating again—eventually, in a few months, down the road a little bit. What was I looking for? Someone who climbed, so we could climb together? Someone stable, stationary? Lots of makeup? no makeup? Liked hip hop? What would she say when I suggested we rent and watch *Serpico* on a Friday night? Had she already seen *Serpico*? Would she care that my car was a piece of shit, and I didn't like to shower that much?

I started scrawling a list on the back of a page of Tommy Riley's boarding pass from his flight to Spokane. It started to run all over the page, sloppy block letters:

TO THE NEXT GIRL:

• I am listening.

• That dress looks incredible on you.

- I will show you the breakbeat in James Brown's "Funky Drummer." I will expect your eyes to light up when you realize that, yes, you've heard that seven seconds of drumming before, in dozens of other songs.

- I will want you to teach me to dance without being self-conscious.

- I will tell you that you are beautiful often, sometimes using the phrase "you are beautiful" or a slight variation, and sometimes I will tell you in more crude, sexual ways.

- I will kiss your forehead, the back of your neck, and sometimes the end of your nose.

- You like to wear backpacks, sleep on the ground, get dirty, and you inspire me to be a more kind, more giving person.

- You are willing to play at least one air musical instrument during car trips.

- You like bears.

- You like to read and will critique/edit the things I write.

- I will want to lie in bed and talk to you before you fall asleep and sometimes after we wake up.

- You are passionate. About whatever.

- I will pick you up at the airport, in a very literal sense. That first hug after I haven't seen you for a few days or weeks will be one in which you are lifted off the ground. I hope that's OK.

- I'm a vegetarian who doesn't drink. It does not bother me one bit if you like to eat rare steaks and drink Jim Beam.

- I will cook for you. It will be more endearing than good.

- I will sometimes listen to the same song 20 or more times in a 72-hour period.

- You will like my parents and find my father incredibly charming.

- You understand what it is like to be in the mountains.

- You are driven. To do something; doesn't matter what.

- You may have some of my ice cream cone, but if you're not that hungry, I'd rather buy two ice cream cones and eat mine plus half of yours. Does that make sense?

- You make me laugh but also laugh at my jokes. But not too easily.

- I will think of you when listening to love songs written about other women, even if the woman's name is the title and/or chorus of the song.

- I am not expecting a woman straight from a men's magazine cover, but I am expecting you to be prepared for a man who thinks you look like a woman straight from a men's magazine cover.

- There are things you can't wait to show me.

- You like to be surprised with gifts.

- You like to be both the little spoon and the big spoon.

- You like bicycles.

- You are OK with having doors opened for you, but believe you should make a higher or at least equal salary to a man who has the same job as you.

- You like coffee shops.

- You don't mind watching movies from the sixties and seventies.

- If your car gets a flat tire, you change it instead of calling someone.

- You like to laugh. A lot.

- You are OK with a man who calls dogs "sweetheart" to their faces.

- You can find beauty in anything.

- You will send me photos because I want to see what the world looks like through your eyes.

- You can learn something from everyone.

- You can be inspired by anything.

- You have real conversations with waitstaff, baristas, and checkout clerks.

- I will never be too tired or too busy or too poor to make you feel loved.

- You will knock me off my feet.

--

At the trailhead for our backpacking trip into Titcomb Basin, there was immediately an issue with how much weight Becca was going to carry in her pack. We would hike 30 miles over five days, almost all of it above 10,000 feet, starting at Elkhart Park. I demanded that she take some of the food out of her pack and give it to me.

"Dude, it's not cool if the pregnant lady's pack weighs more than yours," Fitz joked with me. Fitz had organized the trip as part of a film shoot he was doing for an outdoor apparel company. He was charged with finding "models" to hike around in the company's pants, shorts, jackets and shirts, and I was one of the people he invited. Becca, his wife and business partner, was six months pregnant with their first child.

I had worked for Fitz and Becca for almost three years, periodically writing and recording stories for their podcast series, *The Dirtbag Diaries*. Becca was a focused and direct editor, and I always liked the way my stories turned out through the process of submitting them to Fitz and Becca. Through several re-writes, Becca would push me to write about this or that, take it down this road or that road, and make the story better. We had become friends over the past two years.

The previous winter, Fitz had invited me to a dinner with several climbing magazine editors and photographers, and I remembered the way he talked about his relationship with Becca to all these tough-guy climbers; he had said very directly: "I need her." He was a passionate guy, and I hadn't figured on the dinner conversation turning to love, but no one batted an eye when he said it. I liked that, how unafraid he was to just say that in front of everyone.

I remembered sitting at that table, listening to Fitz, wondering if I needed someone like that. I was happy in my relationship at that time, I thought, but I definitely didn't feel the same way he felt in his marriage—the first word I thought when I thought of Tess wasn't "need." But I brushed it off.

The first time Becca and Fitz met, back in college, she was a little drunk at a party and asked if she could kiss him. He said no. Maybe because his girlfriend was sitting next to him.

Fitz lived on the same street as Becca, and they would occasionally bump into each other as they walked to class. As their relationships broke up and their class schedules aligned, they started to manufacture opportunities to meet for coffee after class—long drinks from the water fountain, packing up their belongings slowly after class ended. Then on a class hike one weekend, they made an early-morning trip to the river in Fitz's truck. Becca rested her head on his shoulder, confirming what they were both feeling.

They spent the summer getting out into the mountains, as Fitz taught Becca how to climb. She had planned to move to Colorado at the end of the summer, long before she had met Fitz; so in September, they said goodbye, and Becca thought, That was that.

Three years went by.

Fitz finished grad school and moved to Flagstaff. Becca came to visit, as friends, for a couple weeks, as she fled a failed relationship and tried to figure out where she would settle for the winter. They climbed together, drank beer, laughed, explored northern Arizona, the same routine they'd had in Washington three years before. At the end of her two weeks in Flagstaff, it was obvious what was happening. But Fitz was finally done with school and was ready for some freedom. Maybe if she went back to Telluride and he stayed in Flagstaff, they could try to see each other more often? It was only a six-and-a-half-hour drive, right? Becca said No, and put her cards on the table. If she was going to try anything, it was going to be staying in Flagstaff. With Fitz.

Fitz went for a run to think about things. Becca walked around the neighborhood, content that she had said what she was feeling, but not sure what would happen. After an hour, Fitz returned.

He smiled. Why don't you stay, he said. So she did.

As we crammed everything in our packs in the parking lot at the Fremont Lake Campground near Pinedale, Becca's pack still felt heavy to me. I took a bag of food out of her pack and put it into mine, to her objections. I did the same thing every day of the trip, as she tried to sneak more and more weight into her pack and carry her share of the group's gear and food.

Three days and 15 miles later, Becca sat out the day of hiking. I asked Fitz if she was OK.

"I think her knee is acting up a little bit, and she hadn't felt the baby kick in almost 48 hours as of this morning, so I think she's worried," he said. Wow. We had spent two nights above 10,000 feet, an elevation that usually messed with people who *weren't pregnant*. You had to stay hydrated, overly hydrated, as well as force yourself to eat just to keep from getting altitude sickness, indigestion, and headaches. Becca had swatted mosquitoes every day and night instead of using DEET bug spray, drank decaf coffee, and slept on a one-inch thick sleeping pad.

I had friends who took nursing pumps to the summit of Mount Hood and on rock climbing outings. I had been passed on jogging trails in the park by eight-months-pregnant women pushing strollers. I did the math in my head and realized that Becca had been pregnant back in April when she and Fitz visited Denver and we went climbing—and she had led some of the pitches. Many of the moms and moms-to-be I knew were heroes, determined to not fall into some barefoot-and-pregnant role.

I was scared of having children. They seemed like a big pause button in life—everything stops, for better or worse, but usually for the better. Important things became less important, and less important things got pushed off your plate. Right? How could I have kids right now, or next year, or the next year? I had so much to do, wanted other things so badly. And I felt guilty about it every time I saw friends and the joy their kids brought to them. Like I'm happy you guys are happy, but I just can't get interested in doing that myself. Right now. Or ever? Ever's a big word. But what if I didn't? Was that OK?

And then I watched Fitz and Becca in the mountains, hiking around with 50-plus-pound packs at 10,000 feet, not slowed down a bit, save the birth classes and doctor's appointments they had to attend back in Seattle when they were home. I wondered how they would adjust when the baby actually arrived and they were three instead of two.

Thankfully, the baby kicked later that day and Becca's knee started to feel better.

At a pass on the trail, we stopped to rest. A man in his late fifties and in great shape chugged up the steep trail under a heavy pack and said hello. As he walked past me, I read his hat: University of Southern California DAD. Did I want one of those hats? Someday? Huh. How do you become a dad who doesn't have a beer belly and only talks about yard work on Sundays? Like that guy.

The stars above the Titcomb Lakes are the best planetarium in the world, a bowl of clear, bright lights hanging above the U-shaped valley with jagged granite ridges lining each side. It was an incredible place. Twelve miles of hiking just to get to the good stuff, the place where Titcomb Basin opened up in front of you and you could just sit there and die and it would be okay.

In two days, my "vacation" would end. I could work remotely from arguably anywhere with an Internet connection. I could head north back to Missoula and drive west to Seattle for a slow trip down the West Coast, as long as it was still fun. Or I could turn south, pick up I-80 in Rock Springs, Wyoming, and head back to Denver. Was I done? Should it be over?

--

Sometimes, going to sleep by yourself again, you just wish you had your best friend around to go for a walk, take her out to dinner, go see a movie—even if you know everything was wrong in the relationship, you just don't want to be sad. And maybe something that's not perfect, not even right, is better than being alone. But you leave it alone, let it go away on its own, and most days are pretty good. Every day, it seems to be a little less, you see the light a little bit and start to think you're going to be OK without her.

But one day, there it is again, in your stomach, hurting for no reason, even though the sun is shining and nothing else is wrong and you're having a good day otherwise. You're just sad. And there is nothing that hurts just like a broken heart does.

My mother loves to watch *A River Runs Through It*, but only part of it. She always shuts it off before Paul Maclean, Brad Pitt's character, dies. She doesn't like the sad part of the movie. I tell her, Mom, art is sad sometimes. And so is life, and life can sometimes be art, even if it hurts your heart so, so bad you want to die. And out here on this highway, I think maybe that's where I am, living this beautiful, sometimes sad piece of art out on the road. I hope so, anyway, because if I'm not, I wonder what the fuck I'm doing out here.

I drive for hours, rolling through the great landscapes of the country to an aspirational soundtrack, and most days, it feels like I'm doing something, that it's all beautiful.

What is a life?

My friend Mark's words bounced around in my head. Is it a family, or is it a comfortable shelter/house/home, or security, or the lack of security? Is it running from all of that stuff, quitting a job, or is it finding work that truly fulfills you? Settling down or picking up and leaving, nesting or traveling? Helping others, helping yourself, reproducing, saving the planet, loving one person or loving everyone you meet or both, finding inspiration or inspiring?

Is life art? That's what I wonder most. Can my life be punctuated by incredible moments, scenes someone would write into a movie script? Can I spend enough of my life in places so beautiful that everyone who passes through gets out their camera to take a snapshot? And if I do, what does that make my life?

An old friend once told me about a New Orleans bartender he had a crush on. Scott said about the guy, "Everything he does is art." I always thought that was the greatest compliment I'd ever heard.

Can I live in a way that looks like art? Can I have a love story that's as good as a fiction writer could create and go places that couldn't be more beautiful if you made them up in your head and painted them on a canvas? And can my heart pound for a few minutes a day with inspiration like I'm at a concert with 80,000 people? When you're talking to me, could our conversation make one or both of us want to change our lives for the better? Can I make you smile, laugh, stop worrying, and start dreaming, just by talking to you and being me?

Is it foolish to try for that, even if sometimes I end up feeling like someone put a spike into my heart, because the sad part is art, too?

--

I could go back to Denver if I wanted to. I could just drive back, put down a deposit on an apartment, and get back to work. Put my toothbrush on the sink in the bathroom, not worry about where I was going to sleep every night.

I was eight hours away. I could take off Saturday and be in Denver by dinnertime, meet some friends at my favorite restaurant, take a shower, and be back in my old neighborhood, getting free coffee from Gio at St. Mark's, settling back in. I could pull my bicycle out of the storage unit, put air in the tires, and fly down the Cherry Creek path at night.

But could I just end it? I felt better about the breakup, yes. It was somewhat uncomfortable living in my car, yes. But even if I was doing nothing, really, but driving around and writing, it felt like I was doing *something*, going *somewhere*. The notes I scribbled on sheets of scrap paper were piling up on my passenger seat, little epiphanies I wouldn't have been having had I been sitting at my laptop in my kitchen in Denver. Would I? I was still almost 3,000 miles short of John Steinbeck's 10,000-mile mark—and that was the minimum number he mentioned.

Steinbeck and William Least Heat Moon were looking for America on their respective trips, looking to satisfy curiosities about the country they called home, but occupied only a small area of in their daily lives. We don't do that anymore, even when we take a big trip. We want to look for answers, look out so we can look inside. Like Kerouac said, the pearl would be handed to me along the way. But I wasn't expecting it to be some a-ha moment, something someone would say to me in a chance encounter, that I would recognize and say, "Yes! There it is. I can go home now. Thank you."

The *New York Times Book Review* published the first review of *On the Road* in 1957. Gilbert Millstein wrote that Kerouac had defined the Beat generation, and that "It is a generation that does not know what it is searching for, but it is searching."

It was a process. My friend Mick had built his log home—not a cabin, but a home—in the woods south of Denver, out of logs he peeled and set himself, not knowing the first thing about peeling logs or home construction before he started. It took him eight years, and I asked him once what he learned from it, besides all the standard construction stuff. He told me it taught him to trust in the process. To keep working and believe that it was all going somewhere in the end. I had stood in that house, heated by a woodburning stove, with its majestic great room lit by the sun coming in the west window, and knew it was something special built by a guy who didn't think he was himself anything special. I thought about that, how he just stuck with it, hoping it would go somewhere.

So I turned north out of Pinedale toward Jackson, then Missoula, aiming for Seattle by the end of the week. After that turn north, it wasn't a vacation anymore. It was a trip, and maybe it would gradually become my life, not just a short break from the norm before I settled back down. I should wander a little bit, follow my nose, trust in the process, because I had never done that before.

Plenty of people have quoted this exchange between Sal and Dean in *On the Road*, but even if it's cliché, it doesn't make it any less true:

Dean: *"Sal, we've got to go and never stop 'til we get there."*

Sal: *"Where are we going to go?"*

Dean: *"I don't know, but we can't stop 'til we get there."*

NINE

I don't need this, I said, digging out a pair of pants and holding them up with the back of the car open on a side street in Seattle's Beacon Hill neighborhood. A climbing guidebook to Glacier National Park, another one to the Tetons. Not going to need those, I said. I stuffed them in a backpack, along with t-shirts I hadn't worn, sweatshirts, a jacket, jeans, socks, extra this, extra that.

I filled three-quarters of a 70-liter backpack, drove to a FedEx store and shipped it to my parents' house in Iowa. I knew they had room for it in their basement. Thirty dollars in shipping is worth it, I told myself, for every time I won't have to shuffle that shit around when I'm looking for a piece of climbing gear or a pair of pants or room to sleep in the car.

I had started the trip with a number of things I knew I needed: climbing gear, backpacks, clothing layers for every situation I would encounter in the mountains—rain, cold, snow—and shoes for every surface and mode of travel—running, walking, rock climbing, snow climbing. I had two shirts with collars and sent one away. Cotton hooded sweatshirt I hadn't worn in two months, also gone. Crampons, staying.

The more you know, the less you need, the saying goes. I don't know where that came from. Possibly a climber who got sick of walking uphill with a heavy pack and decided to take a bunch of stuff out of it.

I read this story in *The Sun* a few years back. This woman wrote that every time she had trouble closing a drawer or a closet door anywhere in her house, she grabbed a piece of paper and wrote down 100 things she could live without, and got rid of them. Did I have 100 things in my car? At least six pens, four water bottles, three stoves, two coffee cups, six pairs of shoes, including two pairs of climbing shoes. Two ropes, 16 cams, two helmets, maybe 40 carabiners? Did I need all that? Could I get by with less?

A few weeks had gone by since I used my rope. But I would need it in a few days, and after that, maybe more often if I headed south to the desert, where the weather wouldn't interfere with climbing. So yes.

Did I need all these pairs of pants? I would typically wear one pair for four or five days, then put on a different pair. I must have had four pairs of pants to climb and hike in — maybe overkill. That didn't bother me. What bothered me was the six or seven pairs of pants I had back in Denver in a storage unit that I was paying $125 a month to keep. The extra computer that

I had somehow lived without for two months while it sat in storage. The small television and DVD player I had kept in our bedroom.

What do we need, really? Most of what was in my car, I needed. Certain things were essential—I needed fuel for the stove, so I could eat. I needed containers to carry water, so I could cook. I needed shoes for my feet. Did I need most of that stuff that was in a storage unit in Denver? Only if I returned and moved into a new apartment. And then what did I need?

Americans love to buy shit. That's what we do. We don't even think about it most of the time. We have disposable income, and we see something, and it's only what, $5, $10? We think it might in some way make our lives better, so we pick it up, rewarding ourselves for having enough money to freely purchase things.

My father has owned several dozen travel coffee mugs over the span of about 10 years, each one incrementally better than the last. My dad uses the newest one, sometimes. Usually it sits in the console of his truck, and every morning, he grabs another ceramic coffee mug out of the cupboard, fills it up, and balances it all the way to work. Once or twice a week, he would walk into the house at 5:30 p.m. carrying four or five ceramic coffee mugs. We are all guilty of this. I must have gotten rid of five travel mugs when I moved out of my apartment, gifts, free with purchase, whatever. None of them worked as well as the $3 one I bought at Pablo's in Denver, and they all just sat taking up space above the refrigerator, moved only when I was trying to get to something behind them.

It's as if we buy things *because we can*. Because capitalism has given us the means to do it. We pick up that new coffee mug. Maybe it will bring us joy. A small amount of joy, something we can believe in. Why would someone make it and sell it to us if it wasn't good in some way?

My friend Jayson, who worked as a political organizer and campaign manager for nearly 10 years, always said, "People don't take time to understand what's wrong with our system and do something to change it, because they're too busy looking at 50 goddamn kinds of cereal and trying to decide which one to buy."

We've evolved into a very high-functioning society, but we have no idea what we actually *need*. We will buy anything: exercise machines that promise to help us look better, gadgets that someone convinces us we need in the kitchen so we can save 30 seconds chopping onions, windshields that sense moisture and automatically send a signal to our windshield wipers to start operating. We have garages and closets and storage rooms in our basements crammed with stuff we've bought and have never gotten around to getting rid of.

Do we have any idea what we actually need? We know what we want, which is more products. More food. More *shit*. We want to buy more and more stuff because we're not happy, and we're not happy because everything we see preys on our insecurities—advertisements and TV shows telling us our boobs are too small, ass is too big, truck/stereo/gun/dick isn't big enough, women will never sleep with you if you pick them up in a car like that, you're not beautiful if your hair doesn't look like that lady's on the cover of *People Magazine* this week, your house is not safe/secure/comfortable. Eat this diet product, buy this Total Gym, get a bigger TV to slowly die in front of. You could have it just a little bit better if you just purchased this product.

When I worked at an outdoor gear store in Phoenix just after I got out of grad school, a guy I worked with wore the same pair of Carhartt pants to work every day. He was a climbing guide and a field biologist in Alaska for a few months every summer. He said to me one day, "I can fit everything I own in a Subaru Outback. And sleep in it." At the time, I didn't know what he was talking about.

Was I happy doing what I was doing, sleeping in my car, everything I needed shoved into a pile next to me? I wasn't checking my bank account to see if I had enough cash to buy a fucking 42-inch plasma TV, that was for sure. I couldn't live in my car forever, but I could learn about myself while I was doing it.

--

Jack Kerouac once stood here, at the end of the two-and-a-half-hour drive from Seattle, a $100 motorboat rental, learning how to drive a motorboat, running it full-blast across Ross Lake for an hour, and five miles of hiking uphill for almost a vertical mile—4,400 feet above the boat dock.

I had known about the hike to Kerouac's former fire lookout for years, always wanting to get there, even though it was so far in the middle of nowhere. If all I wanted was to hang out in a place Kerouac had been, I suppose I could have just flown to New York and walked around the Columbia University campus.

But a true pilgrimage has to have some struggle, right? If there was no pain or suffering on the way there, was there meaning at the end? The hike to the top of Desolation Peak was no shit—three Empire State Buildings' worth of uphill steps. That was suffering enough.

But in the boat, the skies were overcast, the temperature was in the fifties, intermittent rain pelted us, and our movement made its own windchill as the cool air cut through everything in the boat. Teresa's dog, Maile, shivered on the bottom of the boat. I wished I had brought gloves, or at least one glove for my hand that held the boat engine's throttle all the way open for an hour down the center of the reservoir, passing the pine shores and islands on our way to the Desolation Peak Trailhead.

Teresa had yet to read *On the Road* or any of Kerouac's other books, but she was always up for a trip with a purpose, like Desolation Peak. It was a long day, shivering in the boat for an hour, then pounding trail uphill for three hours to get to the short ridge to the fire lookout. The sun came out and warmed us on our way to the summit, but it was still chilly when we stopped hiking at the end of the trail. There it was, unoccupied but unshuttered, like a life-size diorama of a fire lookout's lonely life up there.

In the northwest corner of the 15 x 15 building there was a bookshelf next to the window. I pushed my face up to the glass and looked at the titles: Kerouac's *Desolation Angels*, John Suiter's *Poets on the Peaks*, and three biographies of Kerouac. Most of Hozomeen Peak stood intimidating, a sinister castle to the north, its top third covered by a cloud. The rest of the North Cascades appeared partially or intermittently—the fall clouds had arrived and covered the tops. Lord of the Rings-worthy peaks and football-stadium-sized glaciers popped out where the clouds ended, and I imagined spending eight weeks up there in 1956, or any year, taking in 360 degrees of the incredible mountain scenes.

What did it mean that I was on the summit, where Kerouac had sat a few years after furiously punching out the manuscript for *On the Road*, but a year before the book was actually published and he became famous? I had read *On the Road* when I was so young and had never been anywhere. Now I still hadn't been anywhere, except all around the American West that Kerouac's Sal Paradise was so excited about at the beginning of the book. And I hadn't read the book since I was 15.

Ever since I decided I wanted to be a writer, movement had been what made the words come. Running, walking, hiking, climbing, bicycling—I had gotten a tattoo on the inside of my right forearm three years ago, and all it said, in Courier typeface, was "further." I thought it would remind me where to go, when to go, always.

As summer turned to early fall in Washington, I began to see my trip as a guy frantically writing notes on scraps of paper on a steering wheel, thinking he might have the next Great American Road Trip Book exploding out of him as he pushed the gas pedal down to get to the next place, as if the road itself was blood and had to move through him to make things happen. As if if the road stopped, so would the story.

In the thousands and thousands of pages I'd read, did the one piece of literature that actually meant something to me come when I was 15? Maybe it was this line from *On the Road*:

> *The only people for me are the mad ones, the ones who are mad to live, mad to talk, mad to be saved, desirous of everything at the same time, the ones that never yawn or say a commonplace thing, but burn, burn, burn like fabulous yellow roman candles exploding like spiders across the stars and in the middle you see the blue centerlight pop and everybody goes "Awww!"*

--

"It's a 300-foot hand crack," Fitz said over the phone. When was I going to be in Seattle again, he said, Let's play hooky, go climb Outer Space in Leavenworth on Thursday. Sure thing, I said. We burned through two and a half hours of driving out of Seattle just as the grey skies turned lighter grey at 6:30 a.m., an hour hike and bushwhack to the base of the climb, with mountain goats stalking us, waiting for us to salt rocks and plants with pee so they could eat it. Fitz would lead the hard pitches and give me the good, easier pitches, a selfless act I appreciated.

We simulclimbed the first two pitches, ending at a ledge almost big enough for a car, and Fitz anchored himself to a tree by one piece of rope that someone had left there. It looked solid enough. Fitz is at least twice the climber I am, and he had climbed this route five times, I told myself. Plus this ledge is so huge, a lot of things would have to go wrong to pull us both off of it and send us over the edge a hundred feet to the ground.

He grabbed the gear from me, climbed up, placed a cam, then about 25 feet up, another cam. We talked, joked, made small talk as he moved upward. I was nervous I wouldn't be strong enough to follow the pitch, the 5.9+ section of the climb. It was my first day climbing rock since I climbed Ingalls Peak with Jack a month prior. I was definitely weak, and I was sure Fitz assumed I was way stronger than I was. He had climbed The Nose on El Capitan in a day, something I might be able to do if I dedicated the next two years of my life to training for that and nothing else—no dating, no ice cream, no days off. Fitz was a guy who could legitimately climb and ski with some of the best of them, and had the big, creative brain to make art out of it at the end of the day. And he was going to be a dad in three short months.

Then Fitz was falling toward me from 25 feet up. So fast the first thought I had was to get out of the way.

A husband and a new father, someone who was supposed to come home safe in six hours and be there for Becca in the delivery room in December and for their child's life, had come off the granite, hands and feet whipping through the air around him, nothing but a rope and two pieces of gear keeping him from slamming into the ground below us. And me. Instinct alone locked the rope off in my right hand, but I was sure Fitz's body would hammer into my head and shoulders in another quarter-second, crumpling both of us into a pile on the ledge.

But he stopped, in the air five feet above my head, and we were both instantly apologizing, me for having a little slack in the rope when he fell, him for falling off a route he'd done many times before. The apologies weren't important; what was important was that both his ankles were intact, and that I didn't kill his wife's husband on a Thursday morning playing hooky. And that we both cared. We moved on.

I got to lead all 300 feet of the hand crack, rope trailing out beneath me back to Fitz, and it was as good as everyone had said it was for the past 50 years. I jammed hands and feet into the crack, using the knobs next to the crack as intermittent hand holds and foot holds all the way up, placing protective gear every 15 feet when the climbing was difficult for me and running it out when it wasn't. I was on one of the best rock climbs in Washington, if not all of the Pacific Northwest, a proud tick mark on a list of things to do before I die. It was a gift from a friend.

--

The winding mountain roads in car commercials do not exist anywhere in the United States. Maybe they used to, but there were too many people by the time I got to drive them. If you liked to push the upper limits of your car's handling abilities—barely making it around curves without skidding, tossing your passengers around and making them wish that they, too, had a steering wheel to hold onto—the roads I drove in the West would do nothing but piss you off during the daytime.

Tourists in rental cars, motorcyclists, bicyclists, buses, and cars and trucks carrying climbers and backpackers like me are everywhere now. If you really want to open it up on a mountain road, you'll be interrupted within five minutes, your freedom impeded by one of us going a little slower than as fast as our tires can handle.

National Forest Road 25, between Randle, Washington and Swift Reservoir, Washington, changed that idea for me.

It's 45 miles of pure driving ecstasy, a goddamn rollercoaster of a road built by an engineer who was perhaps motivated by finding the most direct route possible for a road in these parts; but I like to think maybe more so to create something that would bring joy.

I was 16 years old again, behind the wheel of my first car, in love with the freedom of moving myself at a speed faster than my mother would drive, smashing on the accelerator more excited than scared of what it could do, watching the speedometer needle shoot up 20, 30 mph on the short straightaways, punching it in the last half of curves and hoping I didn't have to hit the brakes as I came out the other side. Everything slid around in the back of the car as I flew low around the bends in the road, 20 mph faster than advised on the yellow signs. It was as if an invisible hand were pushing and steering my car faster down the road, skating on blacktop down a tunnel of green so thick you couldn't see the sky.

I ripped it wide open, seeing only five or six other vehicles on the road the entire time.

This is the king, two lanes of speed, gravity, centripetal and centrifugal force, a water-slide bullet-train ride with your hands on the wheel and your own lead foot on the gas. No Estes Park or Yosemite Valley at either end to draw thousands of tourists, no scenic pulloffs to slow you down. Pure American driving for the love of driving. Even for some guy in a piece-of-shit, 4-cylinder, 2.5-liter Subaru Outback with bad tires and a million dents in it, a guy who thought it was over, that there was no joy in driving anymore, who could just as easily be in a BMW Z4 for all he knew. I was almost to Oregon.

TEN

Brian was a little tender, he said, after his second vasectomy

operation in the past few weeks. He and Becca sipped whiskey and wine and

beer around the fire, near Indian Heaven in southern Washington, under the

trees, hardly noticing the intermittent rain. I sat in a camp chair and filled

them in on my trip, my breakup; and we talked about children—my friend

Tim and his 20-month-old son and 15-year-old daughter, Mark and Julia and

their three daughters, Jack and Emelie and no kids, Chris and Natalie and

their chickens-or-kids debate. Brian never wanted kids. Becca was against ever

getting married, but maybe not against having a child.

She and I had met in a writers' workshop at the University of

Montana seven years before, and had clicked immediately, meeting at coffee

shops between classes and having explosively enthusiastic conversations with

lit cigarettes in our hands, as if something needed to be on fire at all times for us to keep the energy going. She had moved to Portland, started working at a bakery, and started her own writers workshop, teaching a couple college classes on the side. Everything I had written and sent somewhere for the past seven years, Becca had read first and given me feedback. I told her that when I got a book published, she'd be the third person to know, after me and the publisher.

The first I had heard of Brian's operation had been in an e-mail five months earlier, when she told me she was writing an essay about it. I read the essay before she submitted it to a couple editors. The first two paragraphs were:

The Short of It

My boyfriend is getting a vasectomy on Friday, and I think I'm okay with it.

The Long of It

When Brian first told me that he didn't want kids we were in bed, golden from the skylight above us. Spider plant shadows brushed across our bare skin. I told him then—and meant it—that it was no reason not to pursue this really good thing that had just begun between us. I was just happy to have a boyfriend for the first time in eight years, to awaken the touch receptors that had been dormant since I graduated from college.

They had a great relationship. They had met through a Craigslist ad, and had their first date at the Oregon Museum of Science and Industry, which they still called "the perfect first date."

Three years into it, they still lay in bed at night and talked until one of them fell asleep.

Their tremendous vegetable garden took up most of the front yard of their house in Southeast Portland, and their living room was nearly completely walled with his-and-hers floor-to-ceiling bookshelves, collections of several hundred books that made you want to grab a cup of coffee and sit down on their couch for a week or two. Becca had recently started taking Poekoelan classes, an Indonesian martial art that Brian had practiced for the past five years and earned his black belt a year ago.

Around the campfire, we talked about the scary stuff: Should you decide whether or not you wanted to have kids before you started dating again? What should you tell women when I went on dates—that yes, I did, no, I didn't, or I wasn't sure yet? Would I meet a woman and just know? I had all these friends who were sure one way or the other.

"And now you know a guy who's so sure he doesn't want kids that he had two vasectomy operations," Brian laughed from across the orange flame.

And Becca had been OK with that. A few days later, at a coffee shop in southeast Portland, I asked her, What do you do, as a woman, when you're getting close to 35 years—do you freak out that you might one day want to have kids and you missed your chance? Her answer was, You look at what you have, not what you might not have.

"Am I going to throw away this incredible relationship I have with another person, just because I think I might want to have a child?" Becca asked. "No. That wouldn't make any sense."

Sure. Why would you take your chances out there again after you'd waited so long for someone perfect? Especially when the relationship was great, so great that you couldn't stop talking to each other even in bed, like two 9-year-olds at a slumber party? Kids were a big deal to everyone, the elephant in the room for me, but that didn't mean everyone was putting so much life gravity on the decision.

What the hell was I doing thinking about it so much anyway? Wasn't it a little bit like worrying about remodeling the kitchen cupboards in a house that hasn't been built yet?

What is a life? If you're happy, it's two people and two cats in a warm house with a garden in Southeast Portland with bookshelves covering the walls, isn't it?

--

The wind blew hard off the bay, rocking my parked car in the driving rain. I couldn't sleep, my legs too long for the back of my car, parked in a rest area just on the Washington side of the Astoria-Megler Bridge, the four-mile truss bridge spanning the Columbia River from Astoria, Oregon to

Washington state, the last link completing the West Coast's great road, U.S. Route 101. When you dream about looking for the big answers in life and being as uncomfortable as possible when you do it, that dream sometimes puts you in a sleeping bag wedged into the back of a damp car in heavy wind and rains. In the morning, I stood in front of a newspaper box reading a headline in the *Daily Astorian*: "Protestors Occupy Seaside" and wondered whether I was missing something or doing something more important.

During my drive to Astoria the previous afternoon, I talked to my friend Mick on the phone, and he said that it sounded like I was having the time of my life, living the dream or whatever. He said he was a little envious, what with the gypsy blood he had. He once took a four-month bike tour to nowhere in particular, to get over a girl. Over the phone, he told me he was postponing a trip to Australia that winter because he didn't want to go for only three weeks instead of six.

I called my friends, sent them e-mails, text messages from wherever I was. I sent gifts for their birthdays, new babies, and sometimes for no reason at all, when I found something in a store somewhere that reminded me of them. They moved and I wasn't there to help carry their couches up the stairs, like I always had been.

When I talked to some of my friends on the phone, most of them said, "Are you ever coming back?" And then things more like, "Well, keep having fun out there. Wish I could go with you." A friend of my parents said,

"I know a lot of guys who would trade places with you." People said words like "adventure," "jealous," "envious," and "living it."

And that felt kind of good. But then, some nights, I was trying to sleep in my car again in some rest area, and I wasn't climbing in a national park, and I wasn't waking up with the sunrise in some campsite somewhere. It was damp and it smelled like a wet dog in my sleeping bag, and the car was about six inches too short for me to actually lie anywhere close to straight up and down. And it kind of wasn't that fun anymore.

I didn't have an apartment or a house to return to, no furniture, no lawnmower, no big TV to spend my Sunday afternoons in front of when I got back. At 32, some days I had a little doubt about what was going on in my life. One day, I looked up the trade-in value of my car, and it was $650. And I was living in it, sleeping next to about $1,300 worth of climbing gear in a Rubbermaid container. I had a master's degree. I had a good job.

I was totally failing at the American Dream of stability, home ownership, a reliable car, or just a mailbox. But was I really failing? Most days, it was pretty good. I got behind the steering wheel, started out for someplace new; the world opened up in front of my windshield; I turned the music up a little, and I had these epiphanies, pieces of essays that I scrambled to write on scraps of paper against my steering wheel, trying to get it down on paper without hitting the semi in the next lane.

From the feedback I had been getting from my friends, I didn't know if the American Dream was home ownership or homelessness, camping and sleeping in your car at rest areas. This is what I said to myself while brushing my teeth in the rain outside the car, watching seagulls hover over the Columbia River as it emptied into the ocean under the bridge. Maybe not homelessness itself, but the freedom I had right now, being able to turn my steering wheel any direction I wanted, and go anywhere I wanted to, because the housing market crash hadn't trapped me anywhere.

Sometimes I thought about where I kept my toothbrush at my last apartment in Denver, in the cabinet 15 feet from my desk and my reliable Internet connection and all my clothes and my refrigerator full of food and my comfortable bed with four pillows on it. After I moved into my car, my toothbrush lived on my dashboard, just under the speedometer, next to my tube of toothpaste. I owned zero pillows.

In his circumnavigation of the Lower 48 in *Travels With Charley*, Steinbeck kept running into people who saw what he was doing and wanted to do it with him, or like him, but were too tied down to houses, jobs, whatever they considered "roots" somewhere. People just wanted to go. They wanted to see about this myth of the freedom of the open road, see what was out there. And maybe many of us still did. Steinbeck set out in 1960 in search of America. My generation, if we go, we wander with the idea of finding something, and sometimes all we get is more lost. Which I guess might be the answer after all.

Twenty-some pages into *Travels With Charley*, Steinbeck stops his camper-truck to get some liquor for his 10,000-mile journey, and the liquor store owner helps him carry a box of bottles out to the truck. The liquor store owner sees the truck and Steinbeck notices "a look of longing" on the man's face. He says to Steinbeck:

"Lord! I wish I could go."

"Don't you like it here?"

"Sure. It's all right, but I wish I could go."

"You don't even know where I'm going."

"I don't care. I'd like to go anywhere."

--

When I met Willis on the sidewalk outside Powell's Books in Portland, he was asleep, and his mother and father kind of seemed like they wished they could have been, too. Ben and Olivia were in town from Los Angeles for a conference Ben was attending. They're young, athletic, good-looking, and financially stable. They climbed Mount Rainier a couple years ago, are both avid cyclists, and were scheduled to climb Kilimanjaro the previous December until Olivia found out she was pregnant with Willis. Ben climbed it, reaching the 19,341-foot summit exhausted, but OK.

Ben is a corporate lawyer in L.A., and Olivia works at a nonprofit. Ben felt some measure of guilt being part of the mainstream, calling himself a "yuppy lawyer," and devoted time and a lot of money to the nonprofit where

I used to work. He's enthusiastic, positive, and engaging, a person you want to be around more. But he and Olivia looked tired outside Powell's that day, almost too tired to smile and give me a hug. They had met online when they were both working in Washington, D.C., a few years before. Olivia said D.C. was "a great place to fall in love," and when she said it, I wanted to meet a girl and fall in love against the backdrop of Woody Allen's *Manhattan*. When they moved to L.A., Olivia was nervous because Ben had walked her to work every day in D.C., and walked her home every day. Heading to the car culture of Los Angeles, she knew they'd both be driving to work, separately, and wouldn't have the 30 minutes of walking and talking together before and after work every day. I didn't want to lose that, she said.

Over lunch and then a cup of coffee, I watched them interact and handle Willis, all of 11 weeks old that day. They were the first parents I'd met who didn't act like they had it all under control, like they knew what they were doing. They'd been doing it for almost three months — I had seen my friend Robb act more confident when we were standing in the neonatal intensive care unit at St. Joseph's Hospital in Denver, less than 24 hours after his twins were born prematurely.

It was refreshing. Ben and Olivia were honest — no one told us about this thing or that thing, they said. You know they talk about the glow when you're pregnant? There is no glow. They had been humbled by a baby. But they concentrated so hard on doing everything right. The first few weeks, they were a bit frazzled. And suddenly I was conscious about walking across a crosswalk in the middle of downtown traffic, like we had a glass sculpture in the stroller. I felt like I should stand off to the side and signal all turning cars to stop right there while we made our way safely to the other side of the street.

I dropped the plush Cookie Monster I had bought at Nordstrom a few hours before into Willis's stroller. He needed good role models, I said. We walked to Ben and Olivia's hotel, The Nines, to grab their bags before they had to grab the shuttle to the airport. It was an incredible hotel, $250 a night, with an atrium on the fifth floor. As we got on the elevator to go upstairs, I thought about sleeping in my car.

Willis was going to be raised in a comfortable home with as many opportunities as Ben and Olivia could give him; and I knew Ben would want Willis to someday be a "dirtbag." Ben had written a little bit about it. He didn't want his son to be poor; he just wanted him to learn the joy of sleeping on the ground, in the car, close to something he loved, which Ben hoped would be in the outdoors—climbing, skiing, surfing, whatever. He wanted Willis to have passion for something, and the ability to choose it, even if it meant giving up being comfortable. I stood there in the atrium of that hotel, looking up at the skylights and manicured plants, and I didn't really know if that's what I was doing, but it felt right.

--

I looked down in my hand one day as I was opening my car door, and I realized I had two keys. One was to my car, the other to a padlock on a storage unit in Denver. Why did I even have the second key? Maybe because when you get down to one key, it feels too small, like you might lose it somewhere if it's not attached to something else, even if all you have is another key.

--

In 2008, I interviewed a guy named Matthew Lee, a mountain bike racer who in 2008, 2009, and 2010 won the 2,745-mile Tour Divide, an unsupported, off-road bike race running from Banff, Alberta to the U.S.-Mexico border along the Continental Divide. He had created the Tour Divide, adding a segment to an already existing 2,490-mile race on the same route.

He was a maitre'd at a resort in North Carolina, and I asked him why every year since 2004 he had taken a month off work in June to ride his mountain bike. He asked me if I had ever heard of the Grand Tour. I hadn't.

The Grand Tour, Lee said, was a tradition for young European men from the 1600s to the 1800s, a rite of passage during which the men would experience the cultures of the continent, experiencing music, art, and aristocratic society. A Grand Tour could last months or years.

"Everybody needs to do a Grand Tour at least once in their life," Lee told me. Americans, he said, were caught up in trying to cram everything into three-day weekends or a few days here and there, and we'd forgotten how to relax, to actually get away and find a different rhythm. You didn't even start thinking differently until you'd been away from work for three days, he said. And when you took a week off work, you just started hitting your rhythm on Day 3, and you had only a couple days of really relaxing before you had to start thinking about going back to work in a couple days.

Was anyone taking a Grand Tour anymore? I could look at a map and point at mountains I'd climbed in what seemed to me a large number of states. But as work had gotten more serious, it felt like I was cramming trips in—leave work at 4 p.m. on Friday, drive six hours to Moab, stay Saturday and Sunday, leave Moab on Sunday at 4 p.m., get back to Denver by 10. Get on a plane after work one day, get dropped somewhere, have fun for two days, cram stuff back in a suitcase that didn't even get unpacked, fly back to Denver, more tired than when I left. I saw places in short increments, snapped photos of the important stuff, then got back to work. Was it like working on a painting one or two brushstrokes at a time, forgetting about it for weeks in between?

Everybody needs a Grand Tour, he said.

I sat with a ceramic mug on the table at Stimulus Coffee in a quiet post-summer-vacation-madness Pacific City, Oregon, looking out the window at a sea stack, waves crashing around it. The ocean couldn't have been more than 300 feet from where I was sitting, breaks rolling up to the beach. I took a phone call, answered e-mails, thought about hitting the road in a few minutes to find a new place to work for the afternoon.

What was I doing killing time in Pacific City, Oregon? Just hanging out? I wasn't here on a vacation, a trip, where there was urgency to see everything on my list or my Lonely Planet guidebook, soak it all up in my mind and my camera before I hurried back to my real life. I had time.

I had time to look at everything, to appreciate the mountains with no names, to walk on the beach for a few minutes, to peek into shops on a Tuesday morning. I wasn't rushing in between all the spots on a list, the most beautiful, the tallest, the most famous. I could drive two hours tomorrow, or I could stay here, or I could drive eight hours and be in California by sundown. It was a new rhythm.

In his book *America,* Andy Warhol says:

Everybody has their own America, and then they have pieces of a fantasy America that they think is out there but they can't see. When I was little, I never left Pennsylvania, and I used to have fantasies about things that I thought were happening ... that I felt I was missing out on. But you can only live life in one place at a time ... you live in your dream America that you've custom-made from art and schmaltz and emotions just as much as you live in your real one.

Was it true that you could only live life in one place at a time?

--

I went down to the beach at Newport to run, but first I did laps on the stairwell that led from the Shilo Inn down to the sand, trying to create some vertical terrain in a flat environment. I ran to keep in shape, not so I could look good with my shirt off. I ran so I would be in shape for the mountains that were always in the back of my mind, the next one, the climb I might do but hadn't picked out yet. The beaches of Oregon were great to run, but flat.

I loved watching the sunset over the endless water that I knew stretched all the way to Russia, looking out over it and knowing how infinite it was, that it could swallow you whole and never give you back; but I was never that moved by the ocean itself. I always made sure to get my feet in it every chance I got, give myself a baptism in it every time I saw it and could walk to it, but I had never surfed, never been in a sea kayak on the actual ocean.

But that was it, the westernmost point on my trip, Newport, Oregon. I had left Denver two and a half months before, driving west, and there I was, out of west to drive into. I was to head south from Oregon, and even if I ended up in Baja, I wasn't going to get any further west than I was in Newport, my feet in the ocean.

The night before, the St. Louis Cardinals had won the National League Pennant, beating the Milwaukee Brewers to go to the World Series. I had called my dad just after the Cardinals made the final out and every

Cardinal fan in America was pumping their fists and jumping up and down in bars and living rooms, including my dad, Joe. I was sitting up in my sleeping bag in my car parked at a pullout on a cliff north of Newport, listening to the ocean roll up the rocks.

I said to myself, I'll always remember where I was when the Cardinals won the pennant: Sleeping in my car. Talking to my dad on the phone.

--

On US 101 in southern Oregon, golden sunlight beamed through the black sea of trunks of shore pine and Sitka spruce, as I slid the car through gentle curves at 55 mph, a controlled fall downhill. The tree trunks whipped past my windows so fast it was hard to pick one out and look directly at it. Then suddenly, the trees stopped and the ocean appeared out my windshield, hundred-foot tall stone monoliths poked out of the water as the waves hammered their feet.

My phone rang just north of Bandon, Oregon, on the coast. My friend Aaron asked, How's your trip going?

I said, Well, it's kind of just become my life now, I guess, and not so much a trip anymore.

You know what you do at the end of a trip? You go home. You go back to all the things you missed while you were away, whether it was your husband, wife, kids, or just your bed. You put your toothbrush back in the bathroom cabinet where it belongs and you sigh and you get grounded again.

So what if you left on a trip and there was no home to go back to? Because that's what I was doing.

He said I'm envious of what you're doing, and I said, It's nothing too fancy, just some dude living in his car, driving around. He said, I'm jealous, man.

I said, Remember that when you're spooning your wife in a nice warm bed and you can get up and make a sandwich whenever you want, and think of me out here crammed in my car, eating macaroni and cheese at some campground by myself. Aaron just laughed.

So much of this you just can't put in a travel magazine or book. You can't promise someone the same reaction you're having to the scenery, to the places you've been. I mean, what would I say? Before you die, drive the Oregon Coast by yourself, but only in the evening, only during an unexpected three consecutive days of sunshine, while listening to the Lord Huron "Mighty" EP. Oh, and make sure your girlfriend or boyfriend leaves you a couple months before you do it, so you're really alone. Would I say that?

Would I ever be in this place again? This was the first time; this is the last time, too. Maybe. Where were the answers? Was I getting close? Was anything *happening*?

ELEVEN

The sun rapidly sank in Crescent City, California, and a ceiling of clouds rolled in over the town as I left, driving south on U.S. 101. I whipped around curves, low clouds blocking the view of the ocean, and I hoped to get to a state park an hour south of town before dark. I liked to at least see a place in the daylight before I camped or parked my car there overnight to sleep in it. Suddenly, the road was 300 feet above the ocean, cliffs dropping away to the right of the car. I was above the clouds, and so was a sunset someone could have put in a painting. Pink dots crossed the sky in latitudinal lines, a pixelated cloud painted by the sun behind it. The cloud ceiling over Crescent City was now the floor of the sunset.

I hit the brakes and turned the car into a roadside pullout, hurrying to find my camera in a climbing backpack somewhere. I fired off a dozen quick photos, focusing on different parts of the sky to make the colors pop, I hoped. A minute later, a man in a pickup towing a raft on a trailer pulled up. He walked toward me with his camera, with a lens that suggested he knew what he was doing more than I did.

"This is worth stopping for, huh?" I asked, smiling.

"Wow," he said. "I was just in the boat, down there, underneath all this, a few minutes ago."

We chatted, Where you from, I'm from Denver, et cetera, and those two minutes were the most I'd talked to anyone all day.

--

This is going to be the first time I've ever swam in the ocean, I said to my friend Amy as we carried rented surfboards down the steps at Pleasure Point in Santa Cruz. I had run on the beach, stuck my toes in the water many times, and my bicycle had been dipped in the Pacific Ocean in San Diego and the Atlantic in St. Augustine, Florida. But I never actually swam in it.

Amy was the creative director for a backpack company and she put her aggressive, funny, born-in-Detroit, raised-in-California personality right in your face the second you met her. I was entertained by the way she talked to everyone, including me. The previous night, we had been out for a trail run near her home in Petaluma, at Helen Putnam Park, and about two miles into it, she said,

"This is where that guy exposed himself to me!"

"Oh really," I said, breathing hard. "Just flashed you?"

"No, the second time he was masturbating," she said.

"Jesus," I said. "Did you just run the other way?"

"I said, 'ARE YOU FUCKING KIDDING ME?'" she said it loud enough while retelling the story to me on the trail that I looked around to see if anyone else was close enough to be offended. She continued, still running, "Then I yelled, 'You're lucky I don't have a can of mace, but I will come after you and KICK YOUR ASS!'"

"And what did he say to that?" I asked, laughing.

"He ran off."

In the kitchen of their house afterward, I met Amy's children for the first time. Ali, 21, was reserved, the calm in the center of the storm. Chris, 20, was funny and vocal, like his mother and father. Chris and Derek, who was 43, acted like they were college roommates. I stood at the kitchen counter eating a falafel wrap and made a comment about its phallic shape, trying to stay on pace with the jokes that were flying around the room like bullets.

"What kinds of foods shaped like dicks are good?" Chris asked.

"All of them!" he and his father Derek shouted in unison.

We left Petaluma at 6:30 the next morning in search of a good beginner spot near Santa Cruz, so Chris could teach me to surf. Pleasure Point was the only place any waves small enough for me were breaking, and about a dozen people lined up in the water a couple hundred feet from the beach. I plowed myself into a rented wetsuit, yanking it up and over my shoulders.

I wobbled just lying on top of the board and paddling out a few hundred feet into the water. This was going to take some learning. Every third wave or so, Chris and Amy took turns giving me advice, pointing out what to look for. Paddle like a shark is in the water after you and when the wave just starts to lift your board, they said, pop up fast, but balanced. Focus on the line running down the middle of your board, stare at it, and use that to figure out your balance.

Then they both yelled at me and talked shit when I fell off. Paddle! Paddle! Harder! Harder! Paddle! Go! I paddled, trying to ease myself into the wave, controlled, but after both my dedication and masculinity were called into question, I began to paddle like a crazy man. I got closer, got a wave underneath me, stood up for a second, maybe a second and a half, and the board squirted out to my left or right and I flopped into the water, tangling myself in seaweed.

I learned to snowboard at age 26, and had been self-conscious and embarrassed. I'd thought I already knew everything I needed to know in life, but then I got humbled by a snowboard, falling and slamming into the slopes every which way for a few weeks while 10-year-olds blew past me. At 32, I knew I wouldn't be a natural at surfing, and that I would learn slowly, so any progress was good progress. Because when do you know everything you need to know and don't need to learn anything new? Can you just sit back and be good at everything? Every fall, I spit out salt water, pulled the board back by its leash and climbed back on again. A dozen or so small waves kicked me off the board, and I managed to stand for a second or two.

"You got up!" Amy said. "A lot of people don't get up at all their first time." I called that a success.

--

Twelve years ago, Amy was a recently divorced, then widowed 33-year-old mother of two at a wedding reception in Fairfax, California, when her daughter Ali introduced her to a guy. Ali was nine, the flower girl, and had been talking to one of the groomsmen, Derek. He was a former Marine, then 31.

Ali ran over to her mom at the reception and said, "Mom, you need to meet him. He's perfect."

Derek took Amy to a quiet side room to talk. He explained that he had known her ex-husband and that he had liked him a lot—not a good start. "That's not the way you hit on somebody, by saying you liked their ex-husband," Amy later said.

Derek was a helicopter pilot, and he told her he had always wanted to take her ex-husband on a helicopter flight before he died. Strike two. Amy hated helicopters, because her ex-husband had nearly bankrupted the family, leaving her under a mountain of debt after the divorce, with his tuition bill for helicopter flight school.

Derek said he wanted to be a police officer. Amy's ex-husband was a police officer. She said, "I don't know if you knew this, but I didn't really like my ex-husband. So this conversation is almost over, unless you can recover."

"Do you want to dance?" Derek asked. Amy said yes. Their first date was the next night. They met at midnight after the Fourth of July fireworks to toilet-paper the bride and groom's house, adding Christmas lights and a handful of pink flamingo lawn ornaments that Derek happened to have in his truck. They set up lawn chairs in the quiet street in front of the house and split a six-pack while they admired their work.

When Chris was nine years old, he asked Santa Claus to make Derek his dad.

Nothing was off-limits in the O'Connell house—the parents gave the kids freedom, and they were good kids. The humor was fast-paced, like being thrown into the middle of a sitcom and trying to keep up with all the jokes. Derek made fun of Chris; Chris made fun of Derek; Derek and Chris made fun of Amy; Amy made fun of Derek and Chris; Ali mostly shook her head and played defense when necessary. They all got along. Their Christmas photos the previous year included one where Chris held a wood saw as if it were his penis and Derek played with it. I wondered who the photographer was, with Amy standing next to Chris, laughing, and Ali covering Amy's mouth with her hand. They competed as a team at the Warrior Dash, an adventure sports race through mud and fire, all wearing purple high-school cheerleading uniforms—Derek and Chris also in girls' uniforms. They were friends, the whole family.

It was only a matter of minutes before someone would say something like, "Brendan, here's something else you probably didn't know about us: We used to have a hermaphrodite bulldog." Violet was a one in 4.5 million chance, an English bulldog with fully functioning ovaries and testes, which was quite confusing for her/him. The O'Connells took to calling her "Violent." When the veterinarian removed the ovaries and testicles, Amy was appalled that he would bill her for both a spay and a neuter. The vet had called a specialist at the University of California at Davis to walk him through the surgery over the phone, and Amy figured, hell, he probably got some measure of fame out of the deal, so why is he even charging us at all?

I wanted to spend Christmas with them. They had a birthday cake made for Jesus, and paid an Irish Catholic priest to come and say mass in their living room, extended family invited. They wore tuxedos and got drunk, only sometimes offending the priest. They referred to it as "Baby Jesus's Birthday."

How did they have such a good family life with such an unorthodox structure? The kids called Derek "Dad" and "Derek." Ali and Chris were better friends with Derek than most children were with their "real" parents. How do you become that parent?

I took off from Petaluma on a Wednesday morning, headed for I-5, planning to cut down the middle of California and get to Las Vegas by Friday and then the North Rim of the Grand Canyon on Friday night. My friend Craig and I had agreed to try to hike and run across the canyon in a day.

--

A Buick pulled up behind my car at a gas station off I-5, and an older gentleman got out and started pumping gas as I waited for my tank to fill and read text messages on my phone.

"That's an interesting bumper sticker," he said. "'How's my climbing?' Never seen one of those before." I told him it was from a guide service in Jackson Hole.

"I'm too old to be doing any climbing," he said.

"You think so?" I asked. "I know a guy who's 87 years old and he's still climbing." This was only partially true. I did not personally know Fred Beckey, but I knew of him, and I knew he was still climbing. My friends Chris and Natalie from Salt Lake City had just run into him on an easy climb near Moab two weeks before. Fred Beckey is my go-to answer whenever anyone says they're too old, too fat, too whatever to go do something crazy like climbing. Eighty-seven years old.

"I won't be climbing anything my motorized scooter can't climb," he said. All right, then. He was simply too old for that shit. He knew what he could and couldn't do, and he wasn't going to have someone telling him he could do something, especially some crazy shit like rock climbing. I didn't know him or anything about his life, but he looked reasonably healthy. He wasn't fucking dead, that was for sure, and I wanted to grab him by the arms, shake him and tell him that. "Well, you're not dead. And if you're not dead, you can do something, right?"

Or should you just wall yourself off from new experiences and concentrate on what you know, what's comfortable? Lots of people are just too old for this shit. Sleeping on the ground, rock climbing, walking somewhere their scooter won't take them, trying something new, going somewhere new, making new friends, losing weight, changing what they eat, leaving home, getting a different job. I would have loved to take my dad on a road trip like I was on, but he had announced that he was too old to be sleeping on the ground about 10 years ago, when he was 50.

Well, was I too old for this? Living out of my car, sleeping on the ground, not showering for days? Maybe I was too old for this nappy haircut, need to put on some closed-toed shoes, start putting some money away. At what point do you become too old for this shit?

Four summers ago, this older guy named Fred sat down across from me at a picnic table near Wonder Lake in Denali National Park, the end point of the bumpy five-and-a-half-hour bus ride through the park's massive wilderness. We ate lunch and talked about our respective trips to Alaska, and about where we were from, the stuff you talk about when all you know about someone is that they're a tourist too, which is obvious there, 85 miles down a private dirt road in one of the wildest places in North America.

Fred was in his sixties, a retired firefighter from Lincoln, Nebraska. He traveled by himself, and I assumed his wife had died, but I hadn't asked. He had driven all of 3,400 miles, including the entire Alaska-Canadian Highway, to get to Denali, a minimum seven-day drive from the Midwest, an adventure any of us would be lucky to ever have the time to attempt in our lives. He camped every other night, he said, stopping at a hotel on alternate nights for a shower and a warm bed.

I loved it, what Fred was doing, and I told him. A lot of people never have the courage to do something like that. I knew people in their thirties who said they were "too old" to camp, to sleep on the ground. Fred said he had a lot of friends who were retired, too, but it seemed like all they wanted to do was sit around and watch golf.

"I told them, you can play golf, that's fine, but you can't sit there and *watch* golf," he said.

Right on, I said, Get out there and live, right? Don't be a spectator.

This retired firefighter, sitting in front of me, in front of the highest mountain in North America towering 18,000 feet above our picnic table, had driven 3,400 miles up there all by himself to see it, 1,400 miles of the trip on one of the wildest roads you can get to from America, and he wasn't being a spectator at all.

I talk to a lot of people who have a lot of limitations—they have back problems, knee problems, too old, too out-of-shape, too busy, would love to do that but we have to stay here in this house or keep this job, don't have the money because we're remodeling the kitchen this year.

Sometimes I imagine Fred having Wednesday morning coffee with a bunch of other retirees in a diner in Lincoln, and he asks the whole group, "Which one of you guys is going to drive to Alaska with me?" And all of them come up with reasons they can't go, and a couple of them crack jokes about Fred, and how he's quote-unquote crazy for wanting to do that, Fred, you're too old for that shit, and Fred goes home by himself. And he sits down at his kitchen table and gets out an atlas like the one I have at home, and he traces the ALCAN with his finger all the way to Fairbanks and imagines Alaska and sitting there and looking up at all 20,320 feet of Denali and he just goes,

Fuck you guys, I'm going for it.

And then he goes down to the basement to see if that old sleeping bag of his is good enough to make the trip, and rubs his chin thinking about what else he'll need to bring along.

--

Twenty-six miles west of Barstow, California, at 8:19 p.m. on October 26, just short of 90 days on the road, I rolled over 10,000 miles. My odometer registered 211,700 miles, and since the odometer recorded 1.1 miles for every real mile of travel, what it thought was 11,000 was 10,000. It was dark. The song on my stereo was "Coastal Brake" by Tycho, which I'd been listening to for over a month since I bought it in Seattle. The lights from two fighter jets from Edwards Air Force Base passed overhead between me and the stars.

Steinbeck set out to cover 10,000 or 12,000 miles in search of America. How many did I need to find what I was looking for? I didn't know, but I liked the ring, the sound of 10,000 miles, and whether or not I'd found whatever I was seeking, I was going to remember when my trip hit 10,000 miles.

I thought about the Grand Tour idea more and more. Matthew Lee had something there. The 17th-century Europeans had it all wrong, though. You didn't need to do a Grand Tour when you were in your late teens. The time to do a Grand Tour was now, when you'd made some mistakes, gotten some scars, some battle damage from life, and you could think about all that stuff out there. But could people do that at my age? Were we all too saddled with obligations by the time we were in our thirties? I was a late bloomer. If I had gone on a trip like this when I was 23, would I have lived the same way, not gotten a mortgage or a car payment, and been free to do this again later? Would I have seen that I could live with less, and avoided the house and the car and the dog and the kids this long?

Everybody needs a Grand Tour. When they need it, I don't know.

--

The Big Dipper was coming out of my belly button, handle down, dipper up in the air, bigger than I had seen it in a while. I lifted my head and looked over my sleeping bag at all the bright desert stars above me, a black ceiling interrupted only by the pink hum of the lights of Las Vegas, about 60 miles northeast as the crow flies. I had driven 12 miles into Mojave National Preserve just after the sunset the previous night on Cima Road, which connects I-15 and I-40 through the middle of the Preserve, across the Shadow Valley, one of the largest and densest concentrations of Joshua Trees in the world.

You might as well drive right down the middle of this road on a Thursday evening, straddling the center line with your tires—you won't see more than a couple other cars, if any. There are no services or towns in the Preserve—a couple campgrounds, but that's it. The Shadow Valley is an otherworldly forest in the middle of a desert that gets less than 10 inches of precipitation per year. The Joshua Trees hang their branches like gnarled fingers along the highway, all sizes, shapes, and designs, and when the sun sets, an orange glow lights the backdrop for these trees and the place looks like Tim Burton drew it. I knew this campsite was here, right across from the Teutonia Peak Trailhead, and pulled off the pavement onto a dirt road, turned in behind a granite dome, and shut the Subaru off for the night. I was maybe 80 feet from Cima Road, but no one could see me.

After dinner, I dropped my sleeping pad on the dirt at the car's front bumper, rolled out my sleeping bag and crawled into it. By the light of my headlamp, I could see small particles of something floating through the air—light rain? Nope, the sky was clear. Dust. It was joy to see dirt in the air instead of the moisture I'd seen in Oregon and Northern California. My sleeping bag would be dry in the morning, and I wouldn't have to leave it spread out in the back window to get the moisture in the down to evaporate.

This was my 39th night in a sleeping bag since January 1, and my 38th night in a sleeping bag since I became homeless at the end of July. It was a $400 sleeping bag, filled with 850-fill goose down, and it only weighed two pounds. I loved it. More than some people love their beds at home. Even when I had a bed, my bed was a place I could wake up in the middle of the night, run out to the living room, and send an e-mail I forgot to send, write something down that I needed to do the next day. I slept with an electric fan running all night to drown out city noises.

Back when I worked at an outdoor gear store, I'd hear people say they couldn't sleep in a sleeping bag, or they'd say things like, "I need to be able to spread out" or, "I get claustrophobic." I always thought they just never taught themselves to sleep in a sleeping bag.

I slept better in a sleeping bag on the hard ground. Did I wake up more? Maybe. It was a different way of sleeping. My sleeping pad was only 20 inches wide, so I had three positions to choose from: Sleeping on my back, sleeping on my left side with my arms folded in front of me, or sleeping on my right side with my arms folded in front of me. The sleeping pad was one inch thick, certainly not a pillow-top mattress with 1,000-thread-count sheets and 10 pillows.

But when I opened one eye, I had Mojave National Preserve surrounding me, bedded down next to this granite dome, a forest of Joshua Trees all around, and a quiet desert wind blowing across my body. And the stars above my head. If I was too hot, I'd pop my head out the top of the bag. Too cold, I'd cinch down the cords so only my nose and mouth were exposed.

You can go to a mattress store and lie down on 30 different beds across a spectrum of prices, pay more for a bed than I paid for the car I sleep in sometimes. If you have trouble sleeping, if you toss and turn, is it really because of the mattress under you? Is there such a thing as a "comfortable bed," or is that just a feeling we have when we're at peace enough to sleep at night?

--

For six weeks, there was a rattling in one of my rear speakers whenever a bass-heavy song played on my car stereo. I figured I had blown it somehow. The speakers were 15 years old, after all. Reorganizing the stove, backpacks, and tent in the back of the car, I finally pried open the speaker to see what was causing the noise, and if I could somehow fix it with duct tape. I turned the car on and played a song. There was the rattle. Rear right speaker?

No, the rear left one. I popped the cover off, expecting a crack in the speaker or something.

It was a pine needle, sitting right in the middle of the dust cap in the middle of the cone. I blew on it, and it flew out into the car. No more rattle. After six weeks. What the shit. I laughed to myself in the middle of the desert, and slammed the door shut.

--

We finally have a house in Colorado so we can start making it feel more like home, a friend wrote on the day she and her husband finished moving from a rented apartment in Colorado Springs to a house they had bought.

I had lived in Colorado for six years, in five different rented apartments. I owned nothing, but Denver felt like home to me more than anywhere else in my life. I couldn't understand what my friend meant, that they couldn't feel at home until they bought, or "bought," a house.

In 32 years, I'd lived at 22 different addresses, and 16 of those had been after I turned 18. Few things survived that many trips in boxes, especially traveling over several states to a new place. But most of those things didn't matter to me so much. What mattered was living near the mountains that rolled like a tidal wave up to Denver's western skyline, and living close enough to escape into them every weekend. In Colorado and the desert in southern Utah, there were places, trails, mountains, campsites, that felt like home. Where I was grounded, where I went when the foundations of my "real life" became unstable.

Three years before, when I was going through my divorce, my worried mother said to me over the phone, "Maybe you should come home for a while and stay with us." Not at all trying to be Hemingway or some sort of stoic, romantic character, I told her I didn't think that was a good idea, and that it would be better if I stayed close to the mountains.

The landscape of my youth, the flat corn country of Iowa, was hard for me—nothing big, ominous on the horizon, no place to dream about going, or wonder what it was like. Just endless fields of corn and soybeans, destined to be mowed down every October and pounded with snow and wind all winter. The mountains and climbing crags where I found myself in my late twenties, that was where I went to sometimes escape and forget about my problems, and, more often, spend time with close friends without distractions.

When things went bad—job situations, relationships, stress, money—I walked into the big hills with my backpack, felt small and concentrated on surviving. I re-amped my senses, deadened from five days staring at a computer screen with the smell of pines, granite tearing at the skin on my fingertips and the backs of my hands, chills I couldn't remedy with the flip of a switch to turn the heat on, the realization that I was only hearing the single sound of a breeze blowing past me in some rock niche where I perched to belay my climbing partner.

When people say "home," they usually mean what's within the walls of a house, where they've hung their pictures, spent Thanksgiving, slept in on Saturdays, swept the kitchen floor so many times that they know exactly how to flick the broom so it pulls the dirt out of that one corner. I don't know why I hadn't had that as an adult.

I didn't grow up in one childhood home—my parents moved around a lot when I was a kid, and I lived in five different towns before I finished high school. A few years after I graduated, my parents left that house for a different town two hours away, and I didn't have a hometown anymore. I couldn't come back to my parents' house for the holidays and run into old friends at a bar or the grocery store. I had a bedroom at their new house, but that wasn't my home either. It was a house where my parents lived, and it was stable and comfortable, but I had few memories there. Every time I went there for the holidays, my grandmother was there, and I always gave up "my bedroom" so my grandmother could sleep in a bed, and I slept on the couch downstairs.

I could say goodbye to an apartment every year or two, no problem. I took the photos off the walls, cleaned the oven, put spackle in the thumbtack holes, and moved on. But I didn't have the heart to leave my neighborhood, leave the characters who showed up at the grocery store at 10 p.m. when I was in there looking for ice cream, leave the quiet streets I ripped down on my bicycle at night, when everyone had gone to bed and I could have them to myself.

My relationship was with the city, and I changed with it. In my neighborhood, restaurants closed, new ones opened, and I remembered what used to be there. I had a story for every business I passed, could remember the time I saw this or that on this or that street corner—a homeless couple getting in a fight, the drunk guy passed out on the sidewalk, a car accident. I saw a certain park bench and remembered having one last talk with my then-soon-to-be ex-wife, and I ran the trails around Cheesman Park and got a little nostalgic for the winter mornings when I religiously pounded out laps at 6 a.m., training for a marathon so I would be forced to quit smoking. I looked for Mount Evans to peek out 60 miles to the west, for just a second, when I pedaled past that one bend in the road at the top of the hill. I looked past all the gay guys cruising in the park, trying to project that I wasn't interested, but didn't mind all the same, that's cool, do your thing. I sat in the beat-up chairs at St. Mark's and wondered how many chocolate chip cookies I'd eaten there and how many cups of coffee the baristas had given me for free in six years, how many tens of thousands of words I'd written longhand in between glances upward at the ever-changing clientele.

My home was not what was under a roof or what was inside a building at the end of a cul-de-sac. I said "home," and I thought of the feeling I'd get after a long day of climbing in the mountains, and, on the way back through the city, I'd hit Park Avenue driving past Coors Field downtown, maybe driving up between the 50-story glass-and-steel financial buildings on 17th and then through the tough love of Colfax on my way to my apartment, just to see what people were doing, what band was playing at the Ogden or the Fillmore, their fans spilling out onto the street. What my city had been doing all day while I was gone, and what it was doing tonight. That was home to me.

Was home. Before I packed all my stuff in my car and left it, without knowing when I was coming back.

I sat alone in a coffee shop, same sort of place I'd been for twelve weeks in two dozen different towns in nine states: Strong coffee, dim inside, big morning and afternoon light coming in through the tall windows in the front. I typed and typed, trying to get the idea of "home" out on a computer, rolling my thoughts together until they said something meaningful, fit a theme or something, made a lick of sense to someone besides me. I glanced out the window every five minutes, staring off into the distance for a second, waiting for the words to come, maybe rubbing my chin like that would help.

Am I looking for a home right now?

Yes. But.

My friend Becca in Portland told me a story about her friend's wedding, that when the officiant interviewed the bride and groom to get some ideas of what to say during the ceremony, she asked the groom what he thought of when he thought of his fiancée.

Home, he said. When I think of her, I think of home.

I put it together in my head in that coffee shop, and I leaned against the wall and stared out the front window at the waning sunlight and the cars rolling by. I'd been homeless for weeks now, but really, it had been forever—*trying* to be in love when it just wasn't quite right, thinking forever might not be so bad with this person even though they're missing this and this and this, we're missing this and this and this.

People spend all this time with real estate agents, looking at all these different houses, trying to find the perfect construction of stairwells and walls and kitchen islands and windows, wondering Do we need a mud room, can we fit our washer and dryer in here, is the yard big enough, are the closets big enough. Do we think this house, these walls, our shelter, will make us happy, or help us be happy. Can we make a life here. Well, what is a life?

--

I missed my turn and made it almost all the way to the west end of Baker, California before I turned off into a gas station to head back, and there they were. I wheeled the car around, and over at the left edge of the parking lot, I looked for a half-second at two women next to a red convertible. They were late-fifties, early-sixties, maybe, taking each other's photos in front of the high desert peaks behind the town as the sunlight faded in the late afternoon. That's all I saw.

Driving back the other way, looking for my turn, I said to no one,

That was *Thelma & Louise*. That was two ladies on a road trip, driving across the desert, just like Geena Davis and Susan Sarandon in that movie 20 years ago, probably one of the most legendary road trip movies ever made, and certainly the most important road trip movie with two female lead characters. And those two ladies I saw, with their red convertible, were out here in Baker, California, because of that movie.

And I said, Yeah, to no one in my car, and I smiled and I laughed, and I said, Those two are a couple of ladies after my own heart.

I was tired sometimes—tired of driving, tired of living nowhere, tired of washing my face in coffee shop restrooms, and I wondered what I was doing out in the middle of the desert, what I was looking for and where it was all going. Thelma, after only a weekend on the road, says:

"Something's crossed over in me and I can't go back. I mean, I just couldn't live."

And she says:

"I don't remember ever feelin' this awake. Everything looks different. You know what I mean ... Everything looks new. Do you feel like that? Like you've got something to look forward to?"

TWELVE

I have never drunk, gambled a single cent, gone to a strip club or a show in Las Vegas. Never been there for a wild bachelor party, never had a limousine pick me up at the airport, never done anything in Vegas that should stay in Vegas, as they say. But I loved to be there, in the middle of all its excess. I couldn't really tell you why I love it. I had been there several times as an adult, always to climb at Red Rock Natural Conservation Area west of the city, or to fly into McCarran airport to start a trip at the North Rim of the Grand Canyon, five hours away.

It is easily the most absurd city in the world. Las Vegas sits in the middle of the desert with no real water source even close, and 2 million people live there running air conditioners most of the year in a sea of concrete. When you fly into McCarran International Airport at night, there's a goddamn pyramid with a beacon of light coming out of the top of it, which can probably be seen from the moon. And inside that pyramid is an elevator that goes up and sideways at the same time—the Luxor's "Inclinator." A friend of mine who went to high school in Vegas described it as the city a little kid would build if you let them—ridiculous architecture, glowing green buildings, an Eiffel Tower crammed right next to the street, a miniature landscape of New York.

What I loved was the way people acted when they were there. I don't imagine another airport in America hears as many squeals and hoots and hollers of anticipation when people de-plane. Another friend who worked in politics in Las Vegas said he constantly met people on his flights back to the city who were dumbfounded that he actually worked there, in Vegas. And also that he wasn't having a drink or several on the Sunday night flight into McCarran.

It's one of the few places in America that somehow gives people a license to act differently, to shed inhibitions, to do things they would never do anywhere else—in Chicago, or Seattle, or Washington, D.C. It's time for a tiny cocktail dress, or getting hammered at 10 a.m., and then again at 3 p.m., and again at 9 p.m. or maybe some recreational drugs, losing hundreds of dollars at a blackjack table, maybe patronizing a sex worker whether or not they have a spouse at home, and in general kind of acting like an asshole. As soon as men across America announce to their closest male friends that they have gotten engaged, probably half of those closest friends announce with wild eyes that the bachelor party will be held in Vegas. There should be a symbolic toilet handle at all the gates at McCarran, that everyone can flush as they exit Vegas onto the jetway of their flight home.

Vegas is what you get when you give America a blank canvas and no rules—sex is everywhere, the opportunity to win money is advertised everywhere; even though we know the house always wins, we think we're special and we'll win big and go home victors, more money than we can put in a suitcase, unlike all the rest of the suckers. For one night or a few nights, women get to dress more glamorously than they can in Kansas City or Minneapolis, and men can feel like high rollers, saying shit like, "What I do isn't gambling. It isn't gambling if you know what you're doing."

Vegas is opulence, if just for a short time. Shooting fully automatic weapons at The Gun Store on Flamingo. Bright lights. Drinks served by beautiful plastic women in tiny dresses. Hunter S. Thompson called Las Vegas "the beating heart of the American Dream," and he had a point.

When you walk down Las Vegas Boulevard, possibility is everywhere: You could meet someone beautiful, maybe love them for just one night. You could eat your weight in Alaskan King Crab Legs. Get married on a whim at a 24-hour chapel. How about a room at the Bellagio? A $4,000 villa somewhere? A hot tub on a balcony 30 stories above the strip? Shows with performers with Olympic-athlete bodies, and no clothes covering them. Girls to your hotel room immediately. Valet parking. I need a drink.

But do we ever feel full or complete when we leave Vegas, the quick fix we thought would help get us back on track? What about the new flat-screen TV in our living room that maybe wasn't worth $1,200 on second thought, the brand-new car that doesn't make us any happier when we're in traffic, Internet pornography, a new hairstyle when we really need to lose 30 pounds to feel better, one more piece of cheesecake because we had a long day at work, another hour of reality television when we really need to sleep instead? Is it sex instead of love, escapism instead of dealing with our troubles, self-medication instead of balance? It's all there in that giant, pulsating, glowing ball in the dusty desert.

I understand it, but I'm not too good for it. I revel in its ridiculousness. Plus, it's the closest airport to the North Rim of the Grand Canyon, where most people start their hike if they're trying to go from the North Rim to the South Rim in one day. Which is what I was going to do with Craig.

--

By the time I picked him up at the airport, it had been a tough week for Craig. The previous afternoon, his son Rob, 23, had flown from Tennessee to Minnesota to check into rehab at Hazelden, hoping it would help pull him out of heroin addiction. A week prior, Craig had called me for advice, the time we should have been talking about what kind of shoes we were going to wear on our one-day, 25-mile, Rim-To-Rim hike and run across the Grand Canyon.

I had been sober nine and a half years, but I told Craig I didn't really know what you could say to someone to help them out. Everybody hits the bottom on their own, and there was really nothing anyone ever said to me that turned me around—I woke up shivering in a jail cell one Saturday morning, and it was my third time in jail, and that did it for me. I said, My dad had once had a 23-year-old son in rehab, so maybe you should call him.

But Craig had wrapped it all up by Friday at McCarran International, all the phone calls, plane tickets, insurance questions, and other arrangements, and he was ready to go down in the canyon.

Craig was 53 and temporarily retired, after a successful career as an executive in the food industry. He was fit, a couple-times-a-year mountain climber, and trail runner, grey hair up top but a face younger than his age. He had not worked for almost three months and was treading water, trying to figure out what was next. We got out of Vegas just before dark, rolling north on I-15 to St. George, Utah, and then to the North Rim of the Grand Canyon, talking about things men don't often understand, such as life and women.

Craig and Tracy had been married for 15 years, after both divorcing from other marriages. Craig had married his then-pregnant girlfriend when they were 19, and after a miscarriage, they stayed married and started a family. By 37, he was unhappy, and met Tracy at work. He told me the story as we drove through the last part of Nevada into the southwest corner of Utah in the dark.

On a business trip, Craig was driving a rental car, Tracy in the passenger seat, two other coworkers in the back seat, and was battling to both drive the car and eat a hurried lunch on the way to an engagement when Tracy fed him a strawberry.

"I said, 'Where have you been the last 20 years?'" he laughed. They were both still married at the time.

"That is such a loaded moment," I said.

And that was it for two marriages that weren't working. They had married when Craig was 39, and he was so happy with Tracy. I always looked at my friends and tried to see myself. What if it didn't happen for me until I was 39? That was seven more years for me, of not finding what I was looking for.

I told Craig about this diagram I had drawn on a piece of paper when I was driving through California a few days before. The diagram looked like this:

Need to work hard

So you can have a stable home/ "security"

So you can raise a family

So they can work hard

And have a stable home/ "security"

↓

∞

And had three questions written underneath it:

1. Is raising a family the most important thing you can do in your life?

2. Does it necessitate a "stable home" and "security"?

3. Are those two things (a stable home and security) the opposite of freedom?

Craig pulled a piece of paper out of the compartment in the passenger door, where I kept all the paper I pulled out when I needed to frantically scribble notes on my steering wheel. He started to draw a diagram, talking as he drew on his knee.

"See, here, you go to high school, that's this box, then you go to college, then you meet a girl, then you get married, then you buy a house, because you need to raise a family, right, then you have four kids," he said, drawing arrows between HS > College > Girl > House > Kids.

"And you have to buy a house," I said. "Because you can't raise kids in an apartment, right?"

"Yeah," he said, drawing a bigger house. "And then, since you got a raise at work, you move into a bigger house, because you can afford it with all the extra money."

"But you get a house with a yard," I said, "because your kids have to have a yard to play in, a grass yard."

"Right," he said.

"And now you need a garage so you can store all the implements to take care of your yard," I said.

"Yes, and this guy who lives next to you, he's a lawyer, and his yard is immaculate," Craig said. "So you can't let your yard look worse than his, so now there's pressure on you to keep it manicured."

"I know, because if your yard looks like shit, the resale value of your house is going to go down, and how are you ever going to sell it for what you put into it? I mean, after it's served its purpose of being a stable home for your kids. Or you decide you need more room."

"Oh yeah," Craig said. "Once your career really starts to get going, you can move into a 4,000-square foot house on three acres, which is what I did. I called that place 'The Echo House.' I'll never live in an Echo House again."

"Right, because it has all those empty rooms?" I said. "And some

Sunday, you have to go to the furniture store to get a sofa and some chairs for that empty room you never use, to fill it up, because maybe when you put furniture in that room, you'll start spending time there, right?"

"Right!" Craig said, laughing.

"No you fucking won't," I said. "When you have people over, you'll still all stand around in the kitchen and tell stories instead of sitting in that comfortable room with all the new furniture in it."

"Exactly," Craig said.

"You know, all this stuff we're talking about, nobody ever told me this when I was young," Craig said.

--

It was 19 degrees Fahrenheit when we got out of our sleeping bags in the dark at the North Rim campground. I crunched granola and dehydrated milk and chugged cold coffee, my fingers stinging in the cold.

We clicked our headlamps off at 6:30, when it lit up around us and the sun was about to peek over the eastern horizon. We started down the trail in shorts and down jackets, wearing thin gloves. At a bend in the trail, I spotted Humphreys Peak, the highest mountain in Arizona, an extinct volcano 50 miles south of the South Rim, near Flagstaff. Even from the North Rim, 60 miles away at dawn, I could see the white of the snow covering its upper third.

We zipped down the trail, taking big, quick steps through the red dirt and rocks, hammered into rough terrain by heavy mules that take tourists down the first few miles of trail. We had 16 miles to cover before we hit the bottom of the canyon, and another nine up and out after that, in 11 hours of daylight. I hoped we were walking at three and a half or four miles per hour to get down, to cover the 5,700 feet of elevation from the North Rim to the Colorado River. After almost three hours of walking, we started to run down the trail in T-shirts.

I bounced on the balls of my feet along the walls of the trail in the Narrows, along Bright Angel Creek, leading into the Colorado River. The canyon pinches down to this for the last few miles, rock walls 100 to 300 feet high, sometimes as close as 40 feet apart, winding down next to the creek until the flats at Phantom Ranch. I was running across the Grand Canyon, the most famous hole on earth, a small backpack bouncing on my shoulders. In my head, with the sound of the creek rushing next to me, I was flying.

"Hey Craig!" I yelled about three miles into the running.

"Yeah?" he looked up, still jogging, trekking poles in his right hand.

"We're running in the Grand Canyon." Craig laughed.

We ran the last seven miles into the cantina at Phantom Ranch, and sat down to drink coffee and lemonade. We ran one more mile over the steel Silver Bridge, one of the only two bridges crossing the river for hundreds of miles in either direction, and watched the water of the Colorado River flowing 60 feet under the steel grid at our feet. After the bridge was eight more miles and 4,400 feet of elevation up the South Rim, through nine different layers of sandstone and 550 million years of erosion.

--

I watched endless desert roll by the windows of the shuttle van taking us from the South Rim back to our car on the North Rim the next morning. Mesas with fluted buttresses lined the horizon, so flat on top like they were leveled off with a ruler, brown and red and pale yellow, and the sun got higher, taking away all the desert's incredible colors and shadows until that evening an hour before sunset.

A variance of a few inches of rain per year in the desert means the difference between a flat of nothing but sculpted sand and dust, and a field of sage and deep green juniper trees. Where the earth creases and channels water through, a 60-foot tall cottonwood tree can grow, its trunk too fat for you to wrap your arms around.

A few years back, my father was driving with my mother and grandmother across the desert east of Las Vegas. My grandmother, who had spent her entire life in the fertile farmlands of the Midwest, looked out the car window and said, "Look at all that wasteland."

Nah, Grandma, that's not wasteland. That's where the magic happens.

Next to me in the van was a couple from Salt Lake City, parents of four kids, and she was a stay-at-home mom. They had taken the weekend off to run the Rim-to-Rim, like we had. They asked where I lived, and I told them I had lived in Denver for the past six years, but I had been living in my car for the past three months.

Do you like what you're doing right now? she asked. I thought for a second, and I said

Yeah,

you know, I do.

I mean, sometimes I think about how nice it would be to be back in Denver sleeping in a bed every night, just being able to call a buddy and say, Hey, let's go get some Thai food at that place we always go to. But when I really think about going back, try to imagine it in my head, going back and settling in, I have to be honest with myself and say it doesn't feel right, not just yet.

Then we started to talk about our favorite places in the desert southwest, all the places I'd been and all the places they'd been and all the places we still wanted to see, and every one of them is a place that a kid from Dipstick, Iowa, would be lucky to see once in his lifetime. Craig was sitting behind me in the van, and this was an incredible four-day trip for him before he had to get back on the plane. I didn't have to get back on a plane. I could go to Joshua Tree after I dropped him off at the airport on Wednesday, go to Death Valley, whatever.

And the lady said, half to me, half to her husband sitting next to her,

There are just so many places we need to get to, and not enough time. And when she said that I thought Yeah, maybe I got a few more months of this left in me.

She asked, what is your favorite place you've been? That's an impossible question, I thought. Did I love Desolation Peak because Teresa was such a great friend to go there with me and because Jack Kerouac is one of my heroes and maybe the reason I was out here in the first place? Did I love the Oregon coast because of the feeling of driving on those cliffsides above the ocean and all the words that spilled out of my head while I was there? The Wind Rivers? The Sawtooths? I couldn't really separate, sitting there in the van, my emotional connection to a place and what it was like, objectively, to be in that place. I couldn't say you'd have the same experience I had. You wouldn't be going there with my friends, and you certainly wouldn't be in the same head space.

I can't tell you how you will feel about a place. All I can tell you are my stories about places.

Sitting in the van, I felt like someone had hit my feet and legs with sticks all day the day before, and when I stood up to walk, it was like I was wearing a 40-pound chain mail suit. Maybe I was still dehydrated, or my body wanted more than nine hours of sleep after the Grand Canyon.

Lots of people did what we had done the day before, probably several hundred every year. Plenty of people did it way faster than we did. I figured if you could run a 10K, you could handle the Rim-to-Rim. But part of me couldn't get over the fact that we walked across the Grand Canyon in less than 10 hours. I looked out the window, music in my headphones drowning out the five other conversations in the TransCanyon Shuttle Van, and knew that might be the last time I walked down in the canyon for a while.

It's an American icon, if not a world icon, and I first saw it on a *Brady Bunch* rerun on TBS when I was a kid. Then I saw it for real, stood up on the South Rim and looked down into it when I was 25, a week after finishing graduate school, and it was huge, a photonegative of a mountain, upside down, dug out of the earth. But I couldn't understand it from up there, like it might as well have been a painting, it was so abstract an idea from 4,400 feet above the river.

I came back, saw it again from the rim, and the first time I walked to the bottom, I was with a friend who was six months in remission from a death sentence of Stage 3 Hodgkin's and non-Hodgkin's Lymphoma, and he battled his way up and out the next day, chemo port still in his chest. Two years later, I climbed a spire just off the North Rim, standing on a sandstone pedestal thousands of feet above the canyon floor, no bigger than someone's living room hanging up there in the dry desert air. Then I came back and took three days to walk across it, down to the river from the North Rim and back up to the South Rim, heavy pack on my back the whole way, watching the sun go down from the bottom of the canyon and wondering if there could be any feeling like it.

And now, Craig and I had shrunk it down, walking and running the whole thing, tackling the Big Ditch in a work day. I had spent more time sitting at a desk in an office on a typical Monday than it took us to get across the canyon. When you take those last steps up onto the South Rim, next to the hotels and restaurants and all the tourists snapping photos, you're safe again, having gone to the bottom and back before the sun goes down, crossed the great river of the Southwest, and climbed out of the largest metaphor in Arizona, and maybe that meant something.

I'd been down in the canyon three times, back out three times, and I'd been all over the West, and I was no less inspired by this landscape than the first time I saw it. Although I had seen so many parts of it a time or two over the past few years, covering 10,000 miles of it in a car, all at once, put it in my blood.

I thought of this quote that longtime Tetons climber Leigh Ortenburger used to have hanging above his desk, from Virgil's *Aeneid*: "All of this I have seen. Some of it I am." Could I say that about half a country, about the West? All these highlighter tracings in my road atlas said Yeah, maybe you can.

At the beginning, I had started on the faith of my own romantic vision of the road, of America's love affair with *On the Road, Travels With Charley, Easy Rider, Thelma & Louise, On the Road Again, Blue Highways, I've Been*

Everywhere, Ramblin' Man, the folklore of

just

going.

I had driven north out of Denver months before, with that one

passage of Kerouac's bouncing around in my brain:

What did it matter? I was a young writer and I wanted to take off. Somewhere

along the line, I knew there'd be girls, visions, everything; somewhere along the

line, the pearl would be handed to me.

Had the pearl been handed to me?

For sure it wasn't a single moment, a person I met, a single place, or

one conversation wrapped up in neat little box so I could stop running and go

home content with it. There was a collection of families, a family made up of

friends of mine, a collection of couples and love stories, none of which were

alike, almost none of whom traced any sort of "normal" map of an American

family.

Over those three months, over 10,000-some miles, I saw the smiles

of my friends who were fathers raising children who were not theirs, the guy

who didn't meet the love of his life until he was halfway through life, the young man running eight miles down a mountain from a fire lookout so he could have more precious hours with that new girl, the couple who fell in love because her kids liked him first. There was something in everyone I knew in Utah, Montana, Washington, Oregon, and California figuring it out as they went, stubbing their toes and tripping sometimes, turning around after false starts and making the second or third try really count, making it as forever as we know how anymore.

I had begun to panic a little at the thought of stopping, setting up in an apartment somewhere, starting a routine, having my stuff all in one place, waking up and knowing where I was. Because people said shit like, "Do it while you're young," or, "Do it while you can," implying that the end was coming, in a few weeks or a few months or whatever, when I got tired, or I finally stopped to settle down.

But all this was out here, huge landscapes to stare out into and scratch my chin and scribble notes on paper, the mountains and desert canyons that made my heart drop in my chest, and the creeks bouncing morning light around the rocks in their beds, and maybe I should do it while I can. Because if you could live anywhere, wouldn't you want to live everywhere? For as long as you could? I mean, really, what is a life, and what is the American Dream, and what is a "home"? The best thing you can do with those questions is keep *trying* to find the answers, not actually find the answers, and tell yourself you have it all figured out and kick your feet up for another weeknight of television.

Off the North Rim, heading northwest on Highway 67, the high-altitude pine forests open up into grassy meadows every few miles, and then the desert comes back as you make your way into Utah, these giant red mesas and peaks dotted with hardy little green trees and bushes. If you time it right, you can drive the back way into Zion Canyon just before sunset, and pop out of the tunnel on Highway 9 and suddenly find yourself a tiny little speck in a car swooping down hairpin turns cut into the 2,000-foot red sandstone walls as you drop into the best place in the world. And I don't know what else to do with the feeling that comes with that besides shake my head and smile at how amazing it all is.

I don't have to go home. I am home.

ACKNOWLEDGEMENTS

Thanks to the many folks who helped with this book, who are all my friends.

Forest Woodward spent hours shooting photos and refused to be paid for his work.

Chris Corkery stayed in touch since the last time I saw him 10 years ago and shared a film he made about his son that made me want to ask him to design the cover of this book.

Hilary Oliver went over and over and over everything about this book with me 15 times and never got tired of helping me shape it.

Pete Hoffmeister read an early version of the first chapter and told me it wasn't ready yet, when I thought it was, and he was right.

Katy Klutznick went through the text with a fine-toothed comb and made it make sense.

Teresa Bruffey was the first person to read the first draft of the entire manuscript and has cheered for me ever since we became friends.

Chris and Natalie, Amy and Derek, Drew and Sarah, Tim and Heidi, Shannon, BJ and Tracy, Brian, Teresa, Sara and Ryan, Abi and Eddie, Ben and Olivia, Steve and Joni, Jarrett and Angie, Syd and Debi, Nick and Emily, Josh and Trinh, Mark and Julia, Lee and Kerry, John and Gay, Mitsu, Bruce and Gerry, Kyle, Becca and Brian, Danny and Tricia, Aaron and Krista, Dan and Janine, and Jack and Emelie all had me as a guest in their homes during the writing and development of the book, and thus became part of it.

ABOUT THE AUTHOR

Brendan Leonard's writing has appeared in *Backpacker*, *Outside*, *Men's Journal*, *High Country News*, *Adventure Cyclist* and dozens of other publications. He is a contributing editor at *Climbing*, *Adventure Journal*, and the podcast *The Dirtbag Diaries*. He lives mostly out of a 2005 Chevy Astrovan in the western United States. More of his writing can be found at www.semi-rad.com.

CPSIA information can be obtained at www.ICGtesting.com
Printed in the USA
BVOW08s1853120314

347473BV00003B/177/P